PUBLISHED VOLUMES

PLANNED VOLUMES

REPENT AND BELIEVE:

The Baptist Experience

in Maritime Canada

Edited by

Barry M. Moody

Assistant Professor of History
Acadia University

PUBLISHED BY

Lancelot Press
for
**Acadia Divinity College and
Baptist Historical Committee of the
United Baptist Convention of the Atlantic Provinces**

1980

ISBN 0-88999-124-3

Published and distributed by
Lancelot Press Limited,
P. O. Box 425,
Hantsport, N. S., Canada BOP 1PO

CONTENTS

INTRODUCTION

It was with the resounding phrase "repent and believe", uttered in pulpits, private homes and even the open fields, that the Baptists built their church in Maritime Canada in the late eighteenth and early nineteenth centuries. In the heat of widespread revival and in the more sober reflections of individual conversions, the Baptist cause spread rapidly in the rural areas, especially among people whose family origins lay in the former Thirteen Colonies. However, as the movement changed from a scattered evangelical sect to a stable denomination it became increasingly clear to many that the simple admonition "repent and believe" was an insufficient base on which to build a self-sustaining organization. Individual conversions were the very foundations of the movement, but, increasingly, collective action was called for if new advances were to be made. It became necessary for both individual Baptists and their churches to come to grips with the growing complexities of a denomination that by the mid-nineteenth century ranked third in numerical importance in the Maritime region and in some areas encompassed more than fifty percent of the population. Issues such as doctrinal orthodoxy, church government, education, class and racial relations, and missionary outreach all required careful, at times, painful exploration and resolution.

The essays presented in this volume explore some of the problems encountered by the Maritime Baptist denomination in the Maritime region in its evolution from sect to church. Variants of these papers were presented at the conference "The Baptist in Canada — An International Symposium" held at Acadia University in October, 1979. This conference, which drew participants and observers from all over North America, was sponsored by the Acadia Divinity College, the Hayward Lecture Fund and the Historical Committee of the United

Baptist Covention, under the very able direction of Dr. J.K. Zeman.

Although the nine essays included here cover one hundred and fifty years in time and many diverse topics, they are nonetheless bound together by the recurring theme of Maritime Baptist identity and definition, as converts found that to "repent and believe" was only a beginning and not an end. George Rawlyk's essay on Harris Harding and the Second Great Awakening explores the broad topic of revival and identity and raises the crucial question of the importance of individual leaders. How a stable and functional church is built on the shifting sands of emotional revival was clearly a major problem faced by the early Baptists. Charles Deweese examines the use of church doctrine and church discipline as vehicles for achieving conformity within both the local church and the broader Baptist community. The Baptist experience was clearly not a uniform one, as geographic, cultural and racial groups faced different individual problems. Savannah Williams examines the struggles of the Nova Scotia Black community to define in its own terms the evolving Baptist Church, which in turn became the major institutional force in the emergence of a sense of Black identity in Nova Scotia.

Esther Clark Wright has drawn upon her more than eighty years of experience of the Maritime Baptist scene to emphasize the significance of the individual convert in the Baptist movement. Frequently without the aid of ministerial leadership, ordinary men and women have defined the directions and shaped the contours of the emerging Baptist denomination. Phillip Allwood's examination of the trials and vississitudes of the Halifax Baptists underscores this point, as well as exploring more deeply the changing Baptist perception of racial, class and doctrinal differences.

The next three essays deal with a common theme, one that became deeply woven into the fabric of the nineteenth century Baptists. My own essay deals with the shifting attitudes toward and perceptions of formal education, setting the stage for the two papers which follow: Allison Trites, in his paper on the New Brunswick Seminary, traces the response to

x

these changes by New Brunswick Baptists, while the impact of evolving concepts of female education is explored in James Davison's essay on the founding of the Grand Pre Seminary.

Perhaps no single topic underscores the changing definition of "Baptist" as clearly as the movement toward union of the Regular and Free Will Baptist groups in the Maritime region. Frank Sinnott examines the doctrinal and structural changes in both bodies that made possible the Union of 1905-06 and the formation of the United Baptist Convention of the Maritime Provinces.

The subjects of identity and definition, of course, have been only partially examined by the papers presented here. Many questions remain unanswered and many areas, only partially explored. The diversity that has characterized Maritime Baptists at times precludes easy categorization. And yet there are unifying themes and underlying currents that make it possible to talk of a "Baptist experience," in a believers' church for which the challenge "repent and believe" has remained central.

Barry Moody

Wolfville, N.S.
February, 1980

From Newlight to Baptist: Harris Harding and the Second Great Awakening in Nova Scotia

G. A. RAWLYK

Contemporaries called the unprecedented outburst of religious enthusiasm which engulfed much of Nova Scotia in 1806, 1807, and 1808 "the Great Reformation."[1] It was not referred to as a mere revival of religion but rather in terms which William G. McLouglin has used to describe profound revitalization movements.[2] It was regarded as being more than a revival; and it was. It was perhaps the most spectacular outward manifestation of one of the most important social movements in Nova Scotia history — the so-called "Second Great Awakening." A principal actor in the unfolding drama of the "Second Great Awakening" as well as a crucial human link connecting Henry Alline's New Light movement with the evolving Baptist Church was the controversial Nova Scotia preacher, Harris Harding.

It is of some interest that so much has been written about Nova Scotia's First Great Awakening and relatively little about the Second Great Awakening. The Second Great Awakening, it may be argued, stretched from 1790 to 1810. There were a number of local revivals in the early period and a more general revival at the turn of the century. Then came "the Great Reformation" of 1806, 1807 and 1808 — the remarkable culmination of the earlier revivals — the spiritual and emotional peak of the revitalization movement.

The First Great Awakening has received a great deal of

1

scholarly attention for three major reasons. First, it occurred at the time of the American Revolution and since so many historians are, and have been, very interested in the Revolution some have focused their attention on the relationship of the Awakening to Nova Scotia's enigmatic response to the Revolution. Second, the First Great Awakening owed a great deal to a single charismatic leader — Henry Alline — who left to posterity a journal, over 500 hymns, a number of sermons, and two major treatises. Alline has, like a giant magnet, attracted scholars. Third, some attention has been drawn to Nova Scotia's First Great Awakening because of what to many is the continuing scholarly preoccupation with New England's First Great Awakening and the relative paucity, until recently, of serious studies dealing with New England's Second Great Awakening.[3]

Nova Scotia's First Great Awakening has been perceived in a variety of ways by different historians and scholars. For Maurice Armstrong the religious revival was simply a "retreat from the grim realities of the world to the safety and pleasantly exciting warmth of the revival meeting, and to profits and rewards of another character."[4] According to S.D. Clark it was basically a "reflection of the collapse of the traditional leadership of the Nova Scotia village communities and the development of a great mass movement of social protest" against the colony's capital, Halifax. The Great Awakening, in other words, was an outsettlement democratic "protest against traditionalism, against authority."[5] For J.M. Bumsted, the "Great Awakening of Nova Scotia was principally a movement of spiritual reform much like those which had over the centuries convulsed Christendom."[6] And as far as Gordon Stewart is concerned, Alline's Awakening was the means whereby many confused and disoriented Nova Scotians resolved their collective identity crisis during the American Revolutionary War.[7] But Alline, according to some of my most recent work, also operated at another level of understanding. Alline preached "the simple, emotional Evangelical gospel of the 'New Birth' and thus provided a powerful new personal and spiritual relationship between Christ and the redeemed believer in a world where all

2

traditional relationships were falling apart."[8]

It seems obvious that each of these interpretations or a combination of them could also be applied to the Second Great Awakening. Yet there are certain dangers in looking for sophisticated explanations of a complex event before that event is understood even at a most elementary or rudimentary level. What is first necessary is to discern in as sensitive and sophisticated a manner as possible the essential anatomy of the Awakening. It is essential to come to grips with the chronology of events and the personalities and issues involved. Once this is done, a few possible explanations may be put forward — but even then they must be advanced in a hesitant and almost reluctant manner.

On December 5, 1806, the Reverend Thomas Handly Chipman, the influential Baptist minister from Annapolis, reported to the readers of the *Massachusetts Baptist Missionary Magazine* that he had been in the Yarmouth-Argyle region for five weeks and that "such glorious times I never saw before." "Multitudes are turned to God," he observed. "I cannot with ink and pen ... describe the one half God has done." Chipman went on:

> Since the work began (three months ago), there have been about one hundred and fifty souls brought to own Jesus, as their rightful Lord and sovereign king .... We have had two church meetings, and surely I never saw such meetings before. It was indeed the house of God, and the very gate of heaven. The last Saturday we began at ten in the morning, and continued until eight in the evening, to hear persons relate the dealings of God with their souls, and then a great number were prevented for want of time....
>
> A great many of the subjects of this work have been young people and children. Seldom a meeting but some are brought to embrace the offers of life; sometimes five, six, and seven at a meeting. There are meetings in some parts of the town almost every day.[9]

Late in January, 1808, the Reverend Harris Harding, who had played a key role in triggering the "Great Reformation," also wrote to the *Massachusetts Baptist Missionary Magazine.* Harding observed that

> Previous to the Lord's pouring upon us the gracious effusions of his Holy Spirit there had been a great declension in religion, attended with great discouragement of soul in believers, and coldness, backwardness, and neglect of religious duties.

"Since the fifth of October last," he went on, "140 persons" had been baptized and "upwards of two hundred persons have been savingly united in Christ."[10] What is remarkable is that the estimated total population of the immediate Yarmouth area was only 1,000. And of this number, some, of course, were Acadian Roman Catholics and others staunch Anglicans.

Harding pointed out that "God has also been pleased to revive his gracious work"[11] to the east of Yarmouth, in the townships of "Argyle and Barrington." It was a region which Harding had frequently visited and he was understandably delighted when his close friend, the Reverend Enoch Towner, could report on April 13, 1807, that in the autumn of the previous year "the Lord had begun his work" in Argyle. As had been the experience in Yarmouth, and would also be the case in other areas of Nova Scotia, the early momentum in the "awakening" was provided by teenagers and some who were even younger. According to Towner:

> The young professors manifested a desire to follow their Lord's commands and to be buried with him in baptism... I was at a loss how to proceed, but resolved ... to hear their experiences.... Nine... (including) seven young converts were baptized... After this the work spread with great power, and people assembled from all parts of the town.... I thought it proper to send for brother Harris Harding ... as he had formerly laboured among them .... ten came forward and was baptized. We both went into the water together, to show that we agreed in heart and

4

practice. The glory of the Lord seemed to overshadow the place, and move on the baptismal waters.[12]

From July 1806 to late October, Towner baptized over 100 people. Then in the early months of 1807, he noticed that the "divine presence" had once again "filled the place — many giving glory to their Redeemer, and many deeply wounded with a sense of their sins." Towner concluded his report by stressing that

> The last Sabbath in March twenty came forward and were baptized. There were five baptisms in the winter season. Twenty-four have told their experiences, who are not yet baptized, and a number of others are under hopeful impressions. The work is still going on in this place, and spreading rapidly in different parts of this province.[13]

One of these "different parts" was Liverpool, a settlement where the Baptists were weak but where the New Lights — Henry Alline's followers — had always been strong and where, moreover, Harding had spent many months over the years preaching his special brand of Christianity. In March, 1807, the Reverend John Payzant, the only ordained New Light Minister in Nova Scotia who had stubbornly refused to become a Baptist, noted that a number of women and young people on the geographical periphery of Liverpool had experienced conversion and were moving from "House to House and telling what great (things) the Lord had done for them." There were nightly meetings and the "young people" were especially active. But the Reverend Payzant was not at all involved at this early stage in what he described as "a wonderful moving (among the people) of the power of God." Finally, on March 3, what Payzant referred to as "the fire" began "to kindle" and "the flame" engulf his Meeting House:

> At night meeting ... as soon as the Sermon was ended the people began to Shout from all sides of the House, either Crying for mercy under a Since of their

parishing condition; or rejoicing and blessing God, for his Goodness to them. The Sinners were cut down by the all mighty power of God, under a Since that there were in a ruined condition, and the Lord has appeared for a number of them, their language was the Lord has appeared and delivered my soul, he has made an everlasting convenant with my Soul. I shall reign with him to all eternity .... and as soon as any one came out, they would call to others to come and partake with them, telling them that there was mercy for them, for they had been the worst of Sinners. And acknowledging all their bad deeds, and if there were any person that they had anything against, they were the first that they went to, and asked their pardon, all offences were made up, and the meeting continued till day. The number that experienced the love of God on their hearts are not yet ascertained. There were more than 20 that came out clear; but it is thought by Some that Stade all night, that there was more than 50 who experienced the love of God.

The next day, by the break of day, the Streets were full of people, of all descriptions, and it appeared that there was ten times as many people in the place as before. So it continued all day they going from house to house. There was no business done that week and but little victuals dressed. The people were So many for there was old and young, rich and poor, male and female, Black and White, all met together and appeared to be as one. At night they came into the meeting House in that manner; the meeting House echo'd with their Praises and rejoicing. So that there was no publick Singing or Prayers but the whole night was Spent in that manner. It was judged that there was above 1000 people.

After the meeting, the assembled throng went from house to house. They were led by "many Small Boys and Girls, Some of

6

them telling the goodness of God, others in distress." Exhausted, conscience-stricken, introspective yet enjoying their unexpected influence and power the young inhabitants of Liverpool continued to witness during the day and to meet together at night. The adults at the evening meeting complained of the constant noise and the yelling. They wanted to hear sermons and, moreover, they demanded order. The young refused to abandon what they considered to be practices sanctioned by the Holy Spirit.

At the end of March, forty-four joined the Church. At that special service, "more than 1000 people" attended. The entire next week "was spent in having meetings, every night, the young people meet[ing] in various places, for they were too numerous to meet in one place." "Whenever a number of them met together," it was noted, "the time was spent Singing Hymns and praying."[14]

The meetings continued until August when Harris Harding arrived. Harding obviously wanted to make Baptists of all the new converts. Payzant vociferously opposed the move and the "Reformation" was replaced by bitter sectarian strife. Some — according to Payzant —were "dipped in bitter water for Baptism;" "It appeared," he spitefully maintained, "that they thought [that] to dip people in water was all the religion that was needful."[15]

At Chester, the Reverend Joseph Dimock noted in his journal that in August 1807

> the Lord made a glorious descent upon the earth against the strongholds of sin and Satan, and caused a great shaking among the dry bones, and bone came to his bone, so that the Sabbath on which the work broke out was concluded with a great shout among the saints, and a great outcry among sinners for mercy .... Our meetings are large, for people throng in great abundance from every quarter to hear.

On the first Sunday in October, twenty people were baptized, including Dimock's wife. Fourteen were baptised on the next two Sundays and by late November "more then forty" had

7

been baptized — "both old and young, male and female."[16]

It is noteworthy that the revitalization movements in Yarmouth, Argyle, Liverpool and Chester owed so much to Harris Harding. Over the years he had carefully cultivated this area and in 1806 and 1807 what was commonly referred to as "the rich harvest of souls" was finally reaped. But in other regions of Nova Scotia considerable life was breathed into the movement by visiting Massachusetts Baptist preachers like Isaac Case, Daniel Merrill, Henry Hale and Amos Allen. Spurred by the events of the Second Great Awakening in New England and inspired by what they knew was occurring in Yarmouth and Argyle, these Yankee Baptists in late 1807 brought what they called "a reformation" to the Baptist heartland located at Horton and Cornwallis and also to the Onslow and Cumberland regions of Nova Scotia.

It seems clear that the "Great Reformation" was of considerable importance in consolidating the position of the Baptist Church in Nova Scotia in particular and the Maritime region in general. The revitalization movement provided the means whereby the revivalistic paradigm first articulated and applied by Henry Alline was appropriated by the Nova Scotia Baptists. In other words, the New Light traditions, significantly shaped by new events and personalities, became the Baptist heritage. And considerable light is shed on this often complex process of transformation by an examination of the fascinating early life and career of Harris Harding.

According to one who knew him, the Reverend I.E. Bill, writing in 1880, Harding's "pulpit talents ... intellectually considered, were never brilliant, but they were generally effective and useful." Bill went on to describe perceptively what he considered to be the strengths and weaknesses of one of the Baptist "Fathers:"

> in the strictest sense, he was an extemporaneous preacher....He deemed it of far more importance that the *heart* should be burning with love, than the *head* should be stored with matter....
>
> If, in addressing a congregation, he never dazzled with the splendour of his eloquence, he often touched

their sympathies, and moved their hearts as he descanted upon the Savior's love....At times there was a melting pathos in his utterances which was overpowering. While there was little method in his discourses, they were generally delivered with fervour, and interspersed with anecdotes illustrative of the topic he was discussing .... As regards religious zeal and activity, every day was devoted to God; and in this respect, his long life was one continuous Sabbath.[17]

For the Reverend E.M. Saunders in 1902,

The dramatic power and element of personal magnetism were effective forces in the personality of the Reverend Harris Harding. [He] skillfully spiced his anecdotes and conversation with a touch of comedy as natural to him as his breath. His imitations of people of peculiar speech were the delight especially of children.[18]

But to one who knew Harding at the beginning of his preaching career, there was little of redeeming value either in his character or in his preaching style. It was Simeon Perkins' contention in 1792 that Harding's "Extravagant Jestures & wild motions of his Body & hands, etc., is, to me very disgusting, and the pain he seems to be in Breath, is distressing." The Liverpool merchant and general factotum later maintained that "a man of his character and principles" should never be permitted to preach the Christian gospel. Harding was, in Perkins' eyes, a dangerous Antinomian who practised what he preached.[19] For example, on September 28, 1796, Harding had been forced to marry — in Perkins' words — "a young woman (Hetty Huntington) said to be pregnant by him."[20]

For his biographer and co-minister at Yarmouth, the Reverend J. Davis, Harding was "an erratic genius."[21] He was "not in every sense a great man" and the "loftier reaches of argument and eloquence were beyond him:"

His utterance was ready, quick, overflowing, apt to be loud and vociferous — in his earlier days accompanied with much gesticulation and movement to and fro.... Deep also was his pathos, abundant his unction, while his tears were frequent....

Out of the pulpit he seemed to live by locomotion. Until arrested by his last sickness he was almost always on the road — alike on the move in winter as in summer .... His capital was not so large as that of some other men; but he kept turning it over and over perpetually, until it had yielded an ample increase, and made its possessor "rich in good works;' superabundant in the fruits of his godly diligence.[22]

And as far as his close associate the Reverend Theodore S. Harding was concerned, Harris Harding "as a preacher was not methodical:"

He dwelt most on the experimental part of religion, and greatly excelled in it. His great forte was 'telling stories.' He was full of anecdotes.

He was eminently useful in the conversion of sinners perhaps more so than any man in this country. He would sometimes seem to prophesy, and mark out people that he though would be converted. He seemed to have an uncommon spirit of discernment that way.[23]

Those who perhaps knew him best, the members of his Yarmouth congregation, described in 1854, the year of his death, his fifty-seven year ministry in the community in the following manner:

For nearly Seventy Years, Sixty of which were spent in this neighbourhood, he proclaimed the Gospel which he loved with unwearied diligence, and extraordinary success.

"And they that be wise shall shine as the brightness of the firmament: and they that turn many to righteousness as the stars for ever and ever." Dan. 12:3.[24]

Harding was born in Horton, Nova Scotia, on October 10, 1761, of Yankee pre-Loyalist stock. Soon after his birth, his parents returned to Connecticut. During the early part of the Revolutionary War, though only a teenager, Harding supported the Patriot side. He was arrested by the British and imprisoned on a man-of-war. In 1783, at the age of twenty-two, and despite his wartime activities, Harding returned to the Horton area with his father. Harding became a school teacher and also attended local New Light services conducted by the Reverend John Payzant, Henry Alline's brother-in-law. In 1783 Payzant and Thomas Handly Chipman were the only ordained New Light preachers in Nova Scotia, aside from Alline; and on the latter's death in 1784, each regarded himself as Alline's logical successor. Payzant would always be opposed to the Baptists, regarding Adult Baptism — as had Alline — as a "non essential."[25] Chipman, on the other hand, had been baptized by immersion in 1779 soon after he had been converted by Alline. If any one man pushed the New Light movement in the direction of the Baptist Church, it was Chipman. He could do it because Nova Scotians knew that he was one of Alline's closest associates; he had crisscrossed the colony with the Falmouth evangelist. Chipman had, in a sense, been legitimized by Alline's success and friendship. He struggled long and hard with Payzant to protect the New Lights from Antinomian "New Dispensationalism" and then when this was accomplished he turned against Payzant in order to create a tightly-knit Baptist Church.

Harding was evidently converted sometime in 1785. He had a profoundly moving conversion experience and he expected that everybody else should share the same emotional ecstasy and the "ravishing of the soul" which he had experienced.[26] Soon after his conversion, he accompanied Payzant in March 1786 to Chester where Harding served as the minister's special exhorter. Harding was obviously being tutored by Payzant and was also being tested in the field.

11

Payzant was a little concerned about his protegé, who had wandered off "with some of old acquaintance ... he had gone with a bad crew." Payzant pointed out in his journal that "I saw what a danger he was in if he gave way to the enemy and Satan like a Roving Lion seeking whom he may devour."[27]

But Harding was not devoured — at least not in the way Payzant had feared. He soon began to itinerate on his own — to Liverpool in 1787, to Chester in 1788, throughout Annapolis County in 1789, to Onslow, Yarmouth and Amherst in 1790 and back to Liverpool in 1791, and to Shelburne, Barrington, Argyle, and Yarmouth.[28] On his travels, Harding did everything in his power to emulate Henry Alline. He tried to look like Alline — according to one contemporary observer "his form was slender, frail, and even ghostly."[29] In later life, however, Harding became quite corpulent, "His length and breadth seemed to be so nearly equal as to suggest ideas of the square and cubical."[30] Harding, moreover, preached Alline's gospel. As far as Simeon Perkins was concerned — and he had often heard Alline — Harding's "Doctrines are much the Same as was propogated by Mr. Alline."[31] Not only did Harding try to cultivate Alline's preaching style and physical image — he even gave the impression at times that he too was dying from consumption — but he also used many of Alline's techniques and he carefully visited those areas where Alline had been successful. Harding, for example, used Alline's hymns and he often explicitly appealed to women and children.[32] And he even attempted to use Alline's imagery and language and wrote many letters to his friends in Horton and Cornwallis, hoping that these letters would eventually be published — thus making him famous.[33] To Thaddeus Harris, he observed from Annapolis on May 14, 1789:

> The Mighty God of Jeshurun has girded his sword upon his thigh, and is riding in the flaming chariot of Israel like a glorious Conqueror: his majesty and power are seen amongst the inhabitants of Annapolis. Some have of late felt his dying groans reach their despairing souls .... I see again the immortal shore that flows with milk and honey....[34]

Harding was determined, as he graphically put it in 1791, to "go in the name of brother Alline's God."[35] When asked once about the publication of his letters "to the Christians," he could only answer — as he put it — "with dear dear brother Alline, God forbid I should write or speak anything but what I would publish, if possible, over the four quarters of the globe."[36] From the declining Loyalist centre of Shelburne he wrote to Thaddeus Harris on August 25, 1791:

> O brother, stand in that gospel that Henry Alline once proclaimed to your soul, and others in Cornwallis. That is the gospel that is the life of my soul, and if I am called to it will not only suffer for, but seal with my blood.[37]

Two days later Harding was planning to follow Alline to New England. "Sometimes I can see a man stand and call," he asserted, "Come over and help us." "I assuredly believe God has called me to preach the gospel on the other side of the flood."[38] But Harding never made his way to New England. Instead, he had to be satisfied with — as he put it — the "general shaking ... the dry bones"[39] in southern Nova Scotia and in writing to Alline's brother in Falmouth. It was a strange yet characteristic letter.

> The lowing of the milch kine is heard in this land. The angel of the Lord is riding on the white horse through Barrington. Three are converted; numbers under great distress, groaning for mercy; and almost every soul is shocked through the place. Jesus also spreads his blessed wings over Argyle; his kingdom is come into three souls in that place, of late, and several are waiting heavily under their guilt. The saints frequently in meeting are crying aloud, 'The sword of the Lord and of Gideon' and righteousness breaks in like an overflowing flood into our Assemblies.[40]

Harding could hardly contain his delight when he was told by one Nova Scotian in 1791 that his preaching was precisely "the

13

Gospel that brought salvation to my soul under Henry Alline."[41]

In common with many of his close associates, Harding "placed great reliance on impressions, and often regarded them as direct intimations of the divine will, which it was his duty to obey."[42] Often he regarded his wish and desire to be the explicit command of the Holy Spirit. It is not surprising, therefore, that Harding became a central figure in the New Dispensation movement which significantly affected the New Light movement in the last decade of the eighteenth century. At the core of the movement were to be found Harris Harding, Joseph Dimock, and James and Edward Manning.[43] According to Edward Manning, after he had abandoned New Dispensationalism:

> Mr. Alline's lax observance of divine institutions fostered in the minds of his followers such ideas as these; that the ordinances are only circumstantials, outward matters, and mere non-essentials; that the scriptures are not the only rule of faith and practice; and that no person is under any obligation to perform any external duty until God immediately impresses the mind so to do.... Several began to question the propriety of having anything to do with external order or ordinances, and soon refused to commune with the church.... As they had no rule to go by but their fancies, which they called 'the Spirit of God,' great irregularities ensued.[44]

In May, 1791, the New Dispensation movement took organizational form and ideological shape in Horton. It was an experience that the Reverend John Payzant would never forget. He noted in his journal:

> The Second Sabbath of May it was the turn to have the Church Meeting and Sacrament at Horton. Mrs. R. rose against all the orders of the Church and [said] that they were but outward forms and contrary to the Spirit of God. These novelties in the Church

caused many to follow the same examples, which made trouble in the Church.... She told me that she had seen the Spirit of God, that baptism and the Lord'[s] Supper, with all Discipline of the Church, was contrary to the Spirit of God and his Gospel, and that marriage was from the Devil, that she was determined to live separately from her husband, for it was as much sin for her to have children by him [as] by any other man and she said that there [were] many that would follow her.[45]

By August, the Church was badly split — "all" was "in Confusion." The supporters of what Payzant called these "fantastical notion[s]" soon "spread from town to town and many adopted this new scheme."[46] The main propagator of New Dispensationalism was Harris Harding, but he was ably assisted by the Mannings and Joseph Dimock. Seeing that the New Dispensationalists were threatening to destroy his church at Annapolis, the Reverend Thomas Handly Chipman, unlike Payzant, proposed a quick counter offensive. He wanted all the New Dispensationalists expelled immediately from the two churches. Chipman felt that unless this was done the New Light Church would quickly disintegrate into warring, bitter factions. Payzant had little enthusiasm for spiritual battle. He was satisfied with waiting for events to determine the future flow of spiritual development in the province. And he escaped to Liverpool in 1793 to get away from the troublemakers in his church. Chipman, on the other hand, went on the offensive. He was determined — as Simeon Perkins cogently expressed it — "to counteract the Antinomian doctrines that have been propagated in this Town [Liverpool] and other parts of the Province, principally ... by Mr. Harris Harding."[47]

By late 1793, it was clear that the New Dispensation movement had peaked and was on the decline, especially in the Horton-Cornwallis region. The Mannings and Joseph Dimock had been frightened and appalled by the Antinomian excesses practiced by many of their former associates. Moreover, the disorder and choas which seemed endemic to the movement appeared to threaten the already fragile

15

underpinnings of Nova Scotia society. Short-term ecstasy was one thing; permanent confusion and disorientation was quite a different thing. The Baptist church polity advocated by T.H. Chipman became increasingly attractive. Joseph Dimock, who had been baptized in 1787, was ordained a minister of the Chester New Light Church on September 10, 1793.[48] It was an ordination endorsed by Chipman and Payzant. Then in the following year, in a controversial ceremony, Harding was ordained as minister of the Onslow Church by his close friend Dimock.[49] Neither Chipman nor Payzant felt able to participate in the ceremony since they felt — as Payzant put it — that Harding "had spoke much against ordination, against ordained Ministers, against the orders of the Church, and many Such like Things."[50] Harding, in other words, was an unreconstructed New Dispensationalist and unworthy of the Christian ministry.

Edward Manning, who was converted under Payzant's ministry in May, 1789, was ordained on October 19, 1795, as minister of the Cornwallis New Light Church.[51] After spending some time in Maine with Baptist preachers and under great pressure from his brother James and Thomas Handly Chipman, Edward was baptized in 1797 by Chipman.[52] A year earlier James Manning had been baptized by Chipman as well; he was ordained two years later.[53] The other "Father" of the Nova Scotia Baptist Church, Theodore Seth Harding, was baptized on May 31, 1795, and ordained at the age of 23 in the following year.[54]

According to Theodore Harding, the Horton revival of 1799 "spread all down till it reached Yarmouth and then Harris Harding joined the Baptists."[55] Harris Harding had first visited Yarmouth in 1790 largely in response to a vivid dream. "I dreamed" he observed

> I was on board a small sail boat, with deacon Cleaveland, and a number of my Christian friends at Horton. Me thought I stood upon the gunwale of the boat, having a spear in my hand. The sun shone with peculiar brightness. We were running before a pleasant breeze, at a little distance from a delightful

shore. The water also was as clear as crystal, and I could see the white and shining fishes at the bottom, while I was continually catching them with the spear. My friends, I thought, were sitting speaking of Christ's love to a fallen world, their cheeks bathed with tears, and apparently filled with peace and joy. I thought the deacon said to me, "You catch every fish you strike." I replied, "I miss none." Methought I fished until I had got the boat filled, and then had a delicious feast with my fellow-disciples. I awoke in a joyful frame. I visited Yarmouth soon after.[56]

The Reverend Jonathan Scott, Alline's formidable foe, was still at Chebogue; he would not leave the province for New England until 1793.[57] While in the Yarmouth region in 1792, Harding helped articulate into existence a revival of religion. There was, he reported on January 27, 1792, "a little cloud, like the bleeding hand of Jesus, in this part of the vineyard." By April, "near fifty ... are savingly born again."[58]

When the revival fires were dampened in Yarmouth, Harding moved on to Liverpool. There were obviously souls to "catch" all along the Atlantic shore. The following year Harding was in the Cobequid region leading a revival there. Then in 1794, as has been previously mentioned, he was ordained at Onslow. The following year he was on the move again, and in 1796 he was in Liverpool. Finally, on May 19, 1797, a distraught Onslow Church "ordered a letter to be sent to call Rev. Harris Harding home.[59] But Harding refused to leave Yarmouth. He had, in all likelihood, moved there from Liverpool late in 1796. In the early months of 1796 Harding had played a key role in bringing about what Perkins called "a remarkable Stir of Religious Concern among people."[60] There was an "Extraordinary stir among the Young People, principally the Females." There were, according to Perkins, much "Swooning and Extices."[61] Harding was exhilarated by the experience; he spent a great deal of time with the young people in the community and some of the young women developed "a great natural fondness for him and thought all his tender expressions for" their "souls was the effect of natural

17

passion."[62] Many young women had felt the same way about Henry Alline. They were sexually and spiritually attracted to men of vigour, decisiveness and elan.

In his relationship with one young woman, however, Harding went beyond the accepted norms of behaviour. Perhaps he was, as Payzant suggested, merely putting into practice his Antinomian beliefs or it may have been that he was trapped into a marriage by a scheming Hetty Harrington.[63] All that is certain, is that under strong community pressure, Harding publicly confessed that he had impregnated the girl. And on September 28 he married her. Six weeks later a child was born to the couple.[64] Harding's supporters, who had wished him to replace Payzant, now withdrew their support. And early in 1797 Harding was called to the Yarmouth Church. He continued to preach at Liverpool in 1797 but only in private houses.[65] He obviously still had his supporters who were willing to forgive a man who was a sinner like themselves but also one who seemed to be a human conduit for the Holy Spirit.

In Yarmouth, Harding "kept school for the support of his family."[66] Influenced by growing Baptist support in other regions of the province, and under considerable pressure from old friends like the Mannings and Dimock, Harding was finally baptized by James Manning on August 28, 1799.[67] A revival was then sweeping through Yarmouth and Manning had "been sent for to assist in the work." Manning described Harding's baptism in the following graphic manner:

> At the time the ordinance of baptism was administered the people looked as solemn as the grave. Mr. Harding's coming to the water seemed like Christ coming to Jordan. After he came from the water he prayed with the people in the street. It seemed as though he had a double portion of the Spirit. Some of the dear christians broke forth in praises to God and the Lamb....[68]

The revival of 1799/1800, although centered at Horton, radiated in all directions — up into the Saint John River Valley, into Cumberland, down the Annapolis Valley to

18

Yarmouth and into Argyle and Barrington. It was obviously a Baptist revival. There was therefore a great deal of truth in Bishop Charles Inglis' report to the S.P.G. in which he warned of "the prevalence of an enthusiastic and dangerous spirit among a sect in the Province called New Lights, whose religion seems to be a strange jumble of New England independence and Behmenism. Formerly they were Pedobaptists, but by a recent illumination, they have adopted the Anabaptist scheme, by which their number has been much increased and their zeal enflamed."[69] Inglis was particularly concerned with Harris Harding's impact. According to the Bishop, intelligence from the Yarmouth area stressed that

> A rage for dipping or total immersion prevails all over the western counties of the Province, and is frequently performed in a very indelicate manner before vast collections of people. Several hundreds have already been baptized, and this plunging they deem to be absolutely necessary to the conversion of their souls. On the Saturday preceding these solemnities the preacher sits above the congregation with a number of select brethren on lower benches appointed to assist him.[70]

Inglis also charged that the Baptists leaders were "engaged in a general plan of total revolution in religion and civil government."[71] Clearly, there was no substantiation for this charge or for Inglis' contention that the Baptist preachers were profoundly influenced by the work of Thomas Paine.

The Anglican Bishop, despite some of the glaring inaccuracies in his report, nevertheless, had correctly perceived the important transformation of many New Lights into Baptists. Concerned about the need for order and discipline, Payzant, the Mannings and Thomas Handly Chipman met in July, 1797, and agreed "to walk together in fellowship as ministers of Jesus Christ" and "to hold a yearly conference, to know our minds, and the state of the different churches standing in connection, by their delegates being sent by them."[72] In June, 1798, the Conference took place at Cornwallis. According to Edward Manning's minutes:

>Mr. Handly Chipman spoke concerning the nature of an Association....Met again at five o'clock. Discoursed largely upon the necessity of order and discipline in the churches, and continued until midnight in observing the dangerous tendency of erroneous principles and practices, and lamenting the unhappy consequences in our churches.[73]

Harris Harding requested admission to the Conference. It was pointed out that he had "deeply fallen into errors" by continuing to espouse the cause of New Dispensationalism. Harding "professed sorrow, humbly acknowledged his offences, signed a document to that effect, craved forgiveness of his brethren, and was received."[74]

Sometime in 1799, the Reverend Thomas Handly Chipman visited Boston to confer with the Reverend Samuel Stillman, the Minister of the First Baptist Church in Boston, about the suit brought against the Reverend Enoch Towner for conducting an illegal marriage. Chipman was also in Boston collecting ammunition for his final assault on the decaying outworks of the New Light Church. At the annual Conference held in 1800, Chipman presented "a close Baptist communion plan."[75] The Reverend John Payzant was furious. When he confronted Chipman, the Annapolis preacher replied "that Mr. Towner had been sued for Marrying and in order to defend the suit he had adopted that plan, that they might be called by some name for they were looked upon as nobody."[76] As Baptists they would have some status in the community; they could stress their link with "the Danbury Association in New England."[77] Without this link and without the name they were without power and influence. It was proposed that the Association name be changed from "Congregational and Baptist," to "The Nova Scotia Baptist Association."[78] The Mannings, Dimock, Chipman, the Hardings and Towner, Joseph Crandall — but not Payzant — accepted their certificates as members of the Baptist Association. It was then agreed by the Baptist ministers present that:

> As many aspersions are cast upon the churches of Christ and the ministers of the gospel, for erroneous principles, etc., the associated ministers and messengers judge it expedient that our church articles of faith and practice should be printed, and the Churches in connection should defray the expense of printing said articles, and the plan of the Association.[79]

Alline's sect, in a sense, had in 1800 become the Nova Scotia Baptist Church.

Chipman's Baptist yoke never rested easily on Harding's shoulders. He resented the growing pressure to exclude from communion those who had not been baptized as adults. He was willing, however, to accept the 1802 Association resolution "that the ordinance of Baptism should not be administered to any but those that join the Churches, except in cases where they cannot be blessed with such a privilege."[80] Harding, it is clear, was not all that interested in Association politics. He was more concerned in 1805 and 1806 with the fact that "the religious aspect in Yarmouth was sadly dark."[81] He must also have been worried about the arrival in 1806 of the Reverend Ranna Cossit, an Anglican minister from Sydney. Cossit was well known as a person who appealed to "the 'lower class' of people."[82] Harding needed some convincing proof that he was indeed doing God's work in Yarmouth. He was thinking about abandoning the ministry unless his "commission...were sealed afresh with tokens of success."[83] He therefore decided to *will* into existence "The Great Reformation."

> Under a strong presentiment of approaching blessing, he ventured to employ language like this: — "Sinners! I have long entreated you to repent and believe. But now I tell you God, by his Spirit, is coming to convince you of sin, of righteousness, and of judgment to come, and convert your souls. Fight against him much longer you cannot; or the Lord

never spoke to me, nor by me — I am a deceiver, and deceived."[84]

Harding — like Alline — was able to use the spoken word as a "bare and brutal engine"[85] against the head and heart of his hearers. His sermons, it was noted, "abounded with short pithy sayings, such as are apt to stick to the memory like burs."[86] There is apparently only one extant verbatim excerpt from one of his early sermons. But this excerpt must have been characteristic of most of his sermons:

> We don't always criticize as heaven will by and by. — The holiness of God is the sinner's torment. —A natural man can no more see beauty in Christ, than a blind man can in colours — If Christ is anywhere, he is in the converted soul — Heaven is a change of nature — True faith is not in the head, but in the heart. —To meet with Christ is more than all the meetings in the world. —Christ in the ordinance makes it sweet. —Christians do more ofttimes to scatter souls from Christ than the unconverted do — Where there's no love, there's no grace. I am going down to the grave. Blessed be God! There is a crown of faith laid up for them that love him. —Unbelief is the worst sin that a man can commit. —If God loves you, he loves you unchangeably. He does not love you for your frames and feelings; he loves you for his name's sake — If you don't love holiness, you don't love God.[87]

At the start of a typical sermon, Harding's manner — it was once recalled — "was still and moderate." But gradually he became more and more agitated. His mind and words began to run off in all kinds of directions. And then his voice became louder and louder and his "speech...rapid and indistinct.... until at length little was heard but a sound, loud, confused and intensely earnest." Next there were "copious tears" and uncontrolled "unrestrained action and movement."[88] For Harding the Holy Spirit was at work. And for many of those

22

who heard him there was a powerful sense of understanding and of empathy with the preacher and the message with which they obviously resonated. Harding was able to create an intense human involvement with the present — with here-and-now existence — as well as with the indefinite, eternal future. His words, and his tears, obviously had a profound impact on his listeners. It was as though his sometimes disjointed words, permeated with intense feeling, captured the essence of the Christian gospel. For many, it was a shattering psychological experience; it was as if the entire New Testament was suddenly uttered in one prolonged Harding sentence. Being powered projections, Harding's words took upon themselves an aura of power.[89]

It was ironic and perhaps only fitting that the man who — according to his biographer — "gloried to the last"[90] that he was a "New Light", first and foremost, and who also found it so difficult to abandon his "New Dispensationalism" should witness the undermining of the "Reformation" by friends putting forward arguments he had used a decade or so earlier. There is a particularly evocative description of these enthusiasts in J. Davis, *Life and Times of the Late Rev. Harris Harding:*

> They had no regard for order or government in the church. Frills, ruffles, all adornments in dress, were their abomination; and they quarreled with Mr. Harding because he would not preach against such things. They brought their peculiarities into the Conference meetings, and warm discussions were held upon them there. They attacked their minister in public, and openly contradicted him. They ascended the pulpit — even the sisters, in the heat of their inspiration — stood at his side — and commanded him to hold his peace. The worship of God was thus changed into confusion and hubbub. Then these people would collect their finery, and commit it to the flames. Some would even take their

crockery and china-ware from their shelves, and bury them. They would enter into minute confession of their sins before promiscuous assemblages. They would form processions in the night, and parade the streets, exclaiming "Behold the Bridegroom cometh! Behold the Bridegroom cometh!" Such were the demonstrations to which these people were led by the spirit that was in them, and which they fondly deemed to be the Spirit of God.[91]

Not only did Harding experience a sickening dose of his own spiritual medicine, he also in 1809 reluctantly withdrew his chuch from the Baptist Association. The precipitating issue was close communion. In 1808, former friends — and New Dispensationalists — argued that in order to ensure continued Baptist growth, it was essential to abandon once and for all open communion. It was contended that "if believer's baptism is the only baptism of the New Testament, those who have been sprinkled in infancy, or afterwards, [were not] lawfully admissible to the Lord's supper."[92] At the 1809 Association meeting held at Cornwallis, the problem was finally resolved. Harris Harding supported open communion, maintaining that the prime concern of the Baptist ministers was to "rely entirely upon that divine influence with which the apostles were favoured when they were setting men apart for the work of the ministry, or building up the church of God" and he "entreated them not to be particular respecting external order or outward forms, which would all perish in the using." Harding was attacked by Theodore Harding who "observed that when the tabernacle was to be erected in the wilderness divine direction was given respecting every part, even for the loops....He considered that the Great Head of the church should be in like manner followed with underrating strictness."[93] This argument was enthusiastically endorsed by the Reverend Henry Hale, visiting Baptist preacher from Massachusetts.

Eventually three churches — Yarmouth, Argyle and Chester — withdrew from the Baptist Association and each of these churches had close ties with Harris Harding. In 1808 there were 1248 members in the eleven Nova Scotia Churches belonging to the Association. In 1809, after the withdrawal, there were only 753 in the eight close-communion Baptist churches.[94] Harris Harding's church had been the second largest in the Association — 250 strong in comparison with Horton's 276. It was not until 1828 that Harding's Chruch was re-united to the Association.[95] In 1811 Chester rejoined and in 1837 Argyle, in somewhat different form, returned to the Baptist fold.[96]

When Harris Harding died in 1854 his church had over 700 members. And a decade later it was calculated that there were more than 2000 Baptists in the Yarmouth region "under the care of *eight* pastors." Harding had found it difficult to die the Christian death.[97] He could not, observed his biographer, "taste those raptures in which he had been wont to luxuriate, regarding them as special proofs of the presence and power of the Holy Spirit."[98] All the old Christian warrior could say on his death-bed was "Good words! good words! But the Lord was not here — the Lord was not here."[99]

It would be a mistake to exaggerate Harding's importance in the fascinating symbiotic relationship connecting Nova Scotia's Second Great Awakening with the transformation of the New Light movement into the Baptist Church. Nor should Harding's role be underestimated. He certainly was not a charismatic religious leader in the Alline tradition. Nor was he an organizational genius in the Timothy Dwight mold. But, it may be argued, he was an important link between the First and the Second Great Awakenings. In a very real sense he succeeded in applying the Alline paradigm of revitalization to another chronological period and to a different mix of people.[100] Harding, in many respects, was a sensitive reflector of the religious aspirations of the thousands of Nova Scotians to whom he diligently preached his highly emotional and introspective version of the Christian gospel. American influences, direct and indirect, events in Europe, economic and social stress in Nova Scotia may have provided the general framework in which the Second Great Awakening worked itself out. Yet without men like Harding, no "Great Reformation" would have been possible; and without him, moreover, the "Great Reformation" would have been quite a different kind of religious movement.

Church Covenants and Church Discipline among Baptists in the Maritime Provinces

CHARLES W. DEWEESE

"The believers' church," as J. K. Zeman has stated succinctly, "strives to practise regenerate church membership." Since Baptists comprise a significant part of the believers' church, they have both stressed and tried to implement a regnerate membership through various ways. Two of the most effective ways at certain times in the Baptist experience have been church covenants and church discipline. This paper will trace the development, relationship and impact of covenants and discipline among Maritime Baptists in the 100-year period beginning in 1778 with the rise of the First Horton Baptist Church in Nova Scotia (now the Wolfville United Baptist Church and Canada's oldest continuing Baptist church). Church discipline will receive more attention than church covenants.

To set the stage — churches used covenants and discipline throughout the period of this study. These two tools for maintaining a regenerate membership had integrated functions: covenants had disciplinary contents, and discipline resulted from covenantal violations. Evidence, however, suggests that while churches continued to use covenants through the 1870s, the disciplinary value of covenants apparently weakened toward the end of this period. Discipline definitely began to experience gradual decline beginning in the 1850s. Reasons for these changes will be described later.

Church Covenants

Role of Covenants in Ecclesiology Maritime Baptists viewed covenanting as integral to the nature of the church. Three examples will illustrate this key point. In a statement printed in 1832 and printed periodically after that by all the Maritime associations up to 1878, the New Brunswick Baptist Association, in a common declaration of faith and practise, asserted:

> We believe that a particular visible church of Christ, is a number of saints and people, by mutual acquaintance and communion, voluntarily and understandingly covenanting and embodying together, for upholding and promoting the worship and service of God, to show forth his declarative glory, and for their own edification.[2]

The 1863 circular letter of the Western Nova Scotia Association related covenants to the obligations of new church members:

> In uniting with the church, each member enters into a covenant with the body, minute and comprehensive, acknowledging his everlasting and indispensable obligations to carry out its conditions. Considering the character of his covenant, and the ground and manner of entering into it, no promises, besides, can be so binding, no pledge so solemn.[3]

This same sentiment was echoed in the 1894 circular letter of the Eastern Nova Scotia Association:

> When *converts* offer themselves to the churches, let them first be duly instructed in the doctrine and commands of Jesus; and then be received into the fellowship of the church, under a full view of covenant obligations, that they may not soon forget their vows, and compel the church to discipline and exclude them.[4]

Uses of Covenants   From the ecclesiological significance given to covenanting, Maritime Baptists moved to the implementation of covenants in church life. Covenants were used in a variety of settings, such as the formation of new churches, baptism, the reception of new members, the Lord's Supper, and church renewal meetings. A good example of a church using a covenant in its formation occurred early in Maritime Baptist life. Although the Horton Church began as a continuing church in 1778, it was initially covenanted between 1765 and 1767. A letter from three members of the church to Elder John Davis, a Baptist in Boston, dated October 27, 1771, stated that Ebenezer Moulton (a Massachusetts Baptist pastor who had moved to Nova Scotia in 1761) had visited the Baptists in Horton in 1765:

> After which & During the stay of the said Moulton with us [he departed in late 1767], we thought it our Duty to Join our selves in Solemn Covenant. And accordingly those who were not Baptized in New England were her[e] Baptized and did sign Covenant together — Hence we Call our Selves the Baptis[t] Church of Christ in Horton in Kings County.[5]

Nearly a hundred years later, on January 23, 1870, in the Falmouth Church in Nova Scotia, baptism, the reception of new members, and the Lord's Supper culminated in a convenantal emphasis.   On that day twelve people were baptized in the presence of many other members. After the baptisms the crowd went to the church and heard a sermon from the pastor. Then the hand of fellowship was extended to the twelve, and the service concluded with the Lord's Supper and the reading of the church's covenant.[6]

Covenant renewal meetings were a part of the records of every Baptist church examined in this study. These meetings tended to be held monthly on the Friday or Saturday before the Sunday in which the Lord's Supper was celebrated. Churches used the meetings to conduct business, carry out disciplinary proceedings, share personal testimonies, qualify those who would receive baptism and the Lord's Supper, and renew covenantal agreements.   Immediately after its formation, the Horton Church began holding covenant meetings on a weekly basis, although they later were held monthly. On the second and third Saturdays of November, 1778, the church met and renewed covenant and then celebrated baptism and the Lord's Supper on the two Sundays which followed.[7] As late as 1862 the minutes of this church recorded that the pastor read the covenant, "and an opportunity was given to all the church members present in rotation, to express their assent to it by speaking or rising. Nearly all present manifested their desire to renew their vows to the Lord and to his people."[8]

While the normal pattern in churches was for the covenant meeting to include covenantal renewal, church business, and disciplinary proceedings, the Horton Church concluded in 1860 that doing all these things in one meeting was "frequently impairing the spiritual character of the covenant meeting by unpleasant, tho' necessary, discussion, and hindering the transaction of business by the hurried manner in which it must be performed."[9] The church then resolved to separate covenantal renewal from church business and discipline by dealing with them on a regular basis in two different kinds of meetings. The church decided to hold its covenant meeting monthly as usual on the Saturday preceding communion and to deal with business and discipline in a quarterly meeting held on Friday.[10] This new approach seemed to work less than a year as quarterly meetings were abandoned and business and discipline were again discussed in covenant meetings.

Summary Covenanting was fundamental to Maritime Baptist life during most of the period from 1778 to 1878 as evidenced by its inclusion in definitions of the church, by multiple uses of covenants, by special meetings focusing on them, and by their close relationship to the disciplinary processes of churches. An example of the significance assigned to covenants appeared in the January 4, 1862, minutes of the Horton Church:

> It would certainly be advisable for each member of the church, in unison with every other, to renew their

covenant with God and with each other, not as a matter of form, but to let the covenant be solemnly read in the meeting. Let all present deliberately rise, and signify their assent thereto. It is a document which, if fully carried out, would answer all our requirements.[11]

Various covenants used were diverse in form and content. Several of the major covenants used were exact reprints of or derivatives of covenants prepared by Baptists in the United States. To illustrate, the covenant used as a model in more Maritime associational records than any other was initially prepared by Isaac Backus for use in constituting the Middleborough, Massachussetts, Separate Baptist Church on January 16, 1756. Backus was the first pastor of the church and renowned advocate of religious liberty and the separation of church and state.[12]

Church Discipline

Discipline will be described as it was reported in four kinds of materials: associational circular letters, other associational documents, conference minutes of the Free Baptists, and church minutes.

Circular Letters   The associational minutes of Maritime Baptists prior to 1878 contained a number of circular letters relating entirely or partly to church discipline. Designed for circulation to all the churches in the associations, these letters helpfully presented disciplinary theory and actual practices. The letters dealing with discipline focused on three aspects of the topic: (1) definition, purposes, and types, (2) cautions, and (3) neglect.

The letters viewed discipline as being both preventive and corrective, although they gave far more attention to the latter. One letter stated forcefully, "A Christian church, in order to preserve the purity, integrity, and growth of its members, must vigorously maintain both preventive and corrective discipline."[13] On the preventive side, several letters urged the necessity of believer's baptism, a regenerate church membership, and care for new converts. After suggesting that many new converts soon became indifferent to the things of God and the church, one letter urged churches to impress upon new Christians the seriousness of their covenantal vows.[14] Another letter expressed beautifully the need to help converts quickly recognize and accept their new responsibilities:

> Don't allow the Christian to feel as that young man, who has come, gloved and slippered into undisputed possession of a large estate, for which another has toiled and sweat, and now has nothing to do but eat, drink and be merry. Rather make him realise that he is a new settler with only a small cleared spot, scarcely large enough to pitch a tent, while broad acres of gnarled forest tree surround him, that if he would enlarge his spiritual possessions, if he would make this soil produce a rich harvest to the glory of God, he must fell these knotty giants of the forest and 'break up this fallow ground.'[15]

The objectives of corrective discipline, according to one association, were to glorify God, to encourage repentance in the offender, to enhance the purity of the church, and to benefit the unconverted by providing a wholesome example.[16] Three letters elaborated on the offenses requiring discipline and on the type of discipline which should be administered in each case.[17] All three letters divided offenses into private and public categories. Private offenses included acts committed wrongfully by one church member against another. The biblical guideline cited for handling private offenses was Matthew 18:15-17. The steps described in this passage were to be followed exactly. Failure to do so brought discipline upon the member making a charge against another member. If a church found a member guilty of a private offense, the church was first to admonish him. If that did not produce a repentant attitude, exclusion was to follow.

Public offenses were those committed against the whole church. These included such things as heretical doctrine, neglect of church duties, and immoralities. Public offenses requiring church action were to be brought before the church as soon as possible. Discipline for public offenses usually involved one or more of four possible responses by a church: private admonition, public rebuke, suspension, or exclusion. Private admonition was considered sufficient in certain cases of indiscretion, especially when the indiscretion had not become public knowledge. Public rebuke was resorted to if an indiscretion had become public. Frequently, serious offenses led to a suspension of church privileges while disciplinary proceedings were in progress. If charges were dismissed, the suspended member was to be restored. If charges were sustained, the offender was usually excluded. Notoriously wicked offenses could result in immediate exclusion on the statement of witnesses.

Although the circular letters were solidly in favor of strict corrective discipline, they also raised cautions about improper use of it. These cautions suggest that there was a kind of pastoral concern underlying the disciplinary process. A key point in the letters was the discipline was not to be simply the task of the pastor but required the involvement of the total membership. Each member's willingness to support and admonish other members was viewed as vital if the learning aspects of discipline were to function effectively in a church.[18]

Another important point in several letters was that churches were to use discipline only with genuine interest in the spiritual well-being of the members being disciplined. One suggested principle was to squelch unnecessary conversation about a disciplinary proceeding.[19] Discipline was to be administered impartially, overlooking family relationships, wealth, education, and influence.[20] Concerning the use of exclusion, one letter cautioned: "every means that the Scriptures will justify, such as prayer, admonition, exhortation and reproof, should be employed for the restoration of a fallen brother, and the church ought not to expel so long as there are any just grounds to hope that the offender may be reclaimed."[21] After members are excluded, however, and show repentance, "we should restore them to our affections and to the Church of God."[22] Churches were to use discipline "with humility, tenderness, zeal, and faithfulness"[23] and to use only those measures based in the Bible and preserving church unity.[24]

Those church members using discipline were further cautioned to examine their own lives. As one association put it, "we think . . . that the acting members in [a disciplinary] case should always be the holiest men in the church and that the voters should be quite certain that they are not themselves guilty of similar offenses."[25] Agents of discipline were also to make certain that their motives were valid. "The exhibition of impure feeling by minister or church," said one letter, "destroys the moral effect of church discipline."[26]

Ironically, even though some rigorous discipline seemed to be practiced throughout the period of this study, circular letters from the 1850s onward dealt repeatedly with disciplinary neglect. Many Maritime Baptists believed that discipline was not prevalent enough. A committee on the state of the denomination, reporting to the Maritime Baptist Convention in 1853, believed that serious inquiry should be made to determine whether the low rate of increase in the denomination could be attributed to a neglect of three areas: insistence on conversion prior to baptism, careful instruction for young converts, and discipline of offenders.[27]

A circular letter of 1880 said, "it is painfully evident that there is among us at the present day great laxity of church discipline" and claimed that this neglect was contributing to a "lamentable degree of ecclesiastical demoralization."[28] The letter continued by recommending a positive and courageous approach to discipline, including a stress on Bible study, prayer, regular self-examination, frequent inspection of the church roll, and appointment of committees to perform careful visitation of church members and families. The letter called for more "moral backbone" in the churches, more scrupulous attention to the requirements of Christ, and a strong determination to carry out corrective discipline as needed.[29]

Potential results of disciplinary neglect were described in various circular letters as placing upon the denomination "the reproach of fickleness of purpose and abandonment of the high vantage ground on which our standard is planted,"[30] helping to "destroy the religious influence of a church, and render inefficient the preaching of the Gospel, and all means of grace that she may employ,"[31] and rendering "ridiculous in the eyes of the world our peculiar principles."[32] As early as 1838 one circular letter raised a provocative question which pointed to the significance of disciplinary neglect: "If discipline be neglected, what distinguishes the church of God from the world?"[33]

Other Associational Materials Associations also dealt with discipline in business sessions, special reports, declarations of faith and practice, and statistical tables. Occasionally, associations disciplined individuals. To illustrate, the June 15, 1798, minutes of the Nova Scotia Association (Congregational and Baptist), formed that year as the forerunner of the Nova Scotia and New Brunswick Baptist Association, noted that a beloved brother, Harris Harding, "who had fallen deeply into error," was present at the meeting with a repentant attitude and had agreed to bring a written acknowledgment of his faults to the association.[34] When the session began on the next day, the following, which illuminates several aspects of an early associational disciplinary procedure, occurred:

Mr. Harding soon brought in his recantation. Being examined and after some little amendments was approved of and the clerk was desired to prepare a certificate signafying [sic] that he had thus acknowledged his faults in principles and practice and that the asociation recommended him to all sister churches while his principles and practices was agreeable to the Word of God. The clerk prepared one and being read was agreed to stand just as specifyed [sic].[35]

Another instance of an association disciplining an individual occurred in 1867 when the African Baptist Association of Nova Scotia excluded Benson Smithers, a pastor, from the association for immoral conduct. The association also voted to annul the credentials it had given to Smithers authorizing him to serve as a pastor.[36] Later, the association apparently restored Smithers and gave him new

35

authority to perform the work of a minister, for associational minutes of subsequent years showed him preaching in various associational meetings. In fact, in 1871, "*It was voted,* That the Rev. Benson Smithers be Bishop of our Association . . . [and] visit the churches once a year."[37]

Associations also dealt with discipline in response to the requests of individual churches. In 1815, for example, the Nova Scotia and New Brunswick Association responded to a disciplinary request from the Chester, Nova Scotia, Church, which asked how to conduct itself toward members who did not attend church ordinances but in other ways lived moral lives. The association concluded that

> such members should be treated with great tenderness, visited, admonished, and prayed for and with; but if such measures prove ineffectual, after suitable forebearance, they should be dealt with as guilty of a breach of the covenant, that is to say that they be excluded from the fellowship of the Gospel.[38]

In 1836 in replying to a letter on church discipline from the First Baptist Church of Halifax, the Nova Scotia Association stated that it had "no intention to interfere with their church discipline . . . unless invited by said church."[39]

Associations also disciplined entire churches. In 1814 the Nova Scotia and New Brunswick Association voted to exclude any church failing to send a letter to the association for three consecutive years.[40] In 1822, after hearing reports from several churches that the neglect of discipline was producing serious problems, the New Brunswick Association "resolved to hold no fellowship with any church that does not strictly observe and maintain, in all cases, those rules of church discipline prescribed and enjoyed by the word of God."[41]

Associations also had articles of faith and practice which related to discipline. The Nova Scotia and New Brunswick Association prepared "Church Articles" in 1808 which recommended both preventive and corrective discipline.[42] The 1832 minutes of the New Brunswick Association contained a declaration of faith and practice
36

which included several references to discipline. The references stressed believer's baptism only, the right of the church "to depose . . . officers who walk contrary to the rules of the gospel; and to discipline their members, though in some cases it may be convenient and profitable to request the advice of neighboring churches", the duty of the minister to "devote himself to the work of teaching, warning, rebuking and exhorting the people publicly, and from house to house", and the responsibility of members to contribute to the compensation of the minister. "Every member deficient in this matter ought to be disciplined by gospel rule, as for any other breach of covenant, or neglect of performing Christian duty."[43] These same disciplinary statements printed early in minutes of the New Brunswick Association were later printed widely in the minutes of many Maritime associations.[44]

Associational statistics also revealed helpful information on discipline. The following table shows the number of people excluded, restored, and removed in churches in various associations for available years:

Association	Exclusions	Restorations	Removals
Nova Scotia and New Brunswick	1810-21 — 226		
Nova Scotia	1822-50 — 1,665	1827-50 — 696	
Eastern Nova Scotia	1851-78 — 811	1851-78 — 308	1851-52 1854-61 — 197
Central Nova Scotia	1851-78 — 1,131	1851-78 — 562	1851-60 — 383
Western Nova Scotia	1856-78 — 1,453	1851-78 — 560	1851-54 1856-58 — 301
New Brunswick	1822-47 — 729	1828-47 — 233	1828-44 1846-47 — 328
Eastern New Brunswick	1848-77 — 893	1848-77 — 349	1848-60 1862-65 — 615
Western New Brunswick	1848-78 — 716	1848-78 — 295	1848-64 — 715
Prince Edward Island	1869-78 — 70	1869-78 — 38	
African Association of Nova Scotia	190 (16 misc. yrs. between 1855 and 1878)		
Totals	**7,884**	**3,041**	**2,539**

All of these figures are based on a careful examination of associational minutes. The statistics show that Maritime Baptists resorted to exclusions, restorations, and removals from the early nineteenth century to well into the 1870s. Since not all churches reported statistics to the associations each year, the actual numbers of exclusions, restorations, and removals were higher than those printed in the minutes. Exclusions from churches in the ten associations totaled 7,884 for the sixty-nine year period 1810-78 (inclusive except for twelve miscellaneous years in which exclusions were not listed or were not accessible). This amounted to an average of 114.3 exclusions per year. The high number of exclusions shows that churches actively employed corrective discipline. It must be remembered, however, that this was only a part of the reformative discipline at work. The associational minutes did not contain statistics on church members subjected to other levels of corrective discipline, such as admonition, censure, rebuke, and temporary suspension.

Still further evidence of corrective discipline was reflected in the removals — usually those whose names were removed from church membership rolls because they had become non-resident members. Removals were listed in miscellaneous years of six associations in the period 1828-65 (though the African Association included them, they are not counted here because they appeared very irregularly and were also ambiguous at times). A total of 2,539 were removed in the period 1828-65 from those churches which reported such action. The same churches in the same period excluded 2,258. Thus, there were twelve per cent more removals than exclusions. This solidly demonstrates that there was little tolerance for the non-resident. To show the combined effect of exclusions and removals, in the random year 1852 there were 16,298 members in the 195 churches in the five white associations.[45] Combined exclusions and removals in the associations for this year totaled 282 (1.7 per cent of the total membership of 16,298 — amounting to 1.4 members per church).

The total number of restorations for the eight associations which listed them from 1827 to 1878 was 3,041 (inclusive except for ten miscellaneous years in which they were not listed or were not accessible). Of the number of persons reported excluded in this period, 42.75 per cent were restored (based on a comparison of all the minutes in the eight associations for which both exclusions and restorations were listed). Thus, churches did express some measure of concern for former members who had undergone corrective discipline.

Free Baptist Conferences: Not only did Baptist associations deal with discipline, the Free Baptist conferences also gave it attention. An 1848 statement of beliefs of the Free Christian Baptists in Nova Scotia and New Brunswick contained an article on the duties of churches, one of which was "the exercise of church discipline."[46] This same confession appeared later in the minutes of at least two conference meetings of Free Baptists in New Brunswick (1857 and 1864) and one such meeting in Nova Scotia (1866).[47]

A statement of church usages appeared in the 1855 and 1864 minutes of the Free Christian Baptist General Conference of New Brunswick. Article VII on "Church Discipline" said:

> Cases of discipline after private admonition and counsel by the Pastor or some other officer of the church, shall be brought before the Officers' Meeting, and the parties shall be considered as suspended from church privileges until reclaimed, but sentence of excommunication shall be the act of the Church Meeting only.[48]

The same church usages, including this statement on discipline, were to be read at every monthly conference meeting in churches and more often when practical.[49] This disciplinary statement with only minor variations appeared in the 1866 and 1877 minutes of the Free Baptist Conference of Nova Scotia with the indication that all the church usages should be read in church conference at least once every three months.[50]

The 1868 church directory of the Free Christian Baptist General Conference of New Brunswick contained much more material on discipline.[51] Baptism was for believers only, and persons desiring admission into churches had to give credible evidence of their regeneration. In private offenses church officers were to make sure that the guidelines of Matthew 18 had been followed before hearing a case. Public offenses required private admonition by the pastor or some other officer, a hearing in a meeting of church officers, and a suspension of the guilty from church privileges until reclaimed. After hearing a case the officers could make specific recommendations to the church, but only the church could exclude someone from membership. One exception was that with "adultery or any high crime" the officers could exclude transgressors if they had sufficient evidence.

According to the Free Baptist directory, three important disciplinary relationships existed between the district meetings, on the one hand, and churches and/or individual members of churches, on the other. First, in a case where divisiveness or some other problem became such a predominant feature of a church's life that the church could not help itself, the district meeting to which the church belonged had the power "to take charge of the Church, and in its care and labor for its good, exercise such discipline as it may think necessary."[52] Second, if any portion of a church became disloyal to the doctrines, polity, or constitution of the denomination, the district meeting could "acknowledge and sustain as the Church those members who shall be found loyal to the denomination; and further, if it be deemed necessary, it shall have the power to reorganize such members into a Church, which shall bear the name and date of the original organization."[53] Third, "Disciplined persons who may feel aggrieved with the decision of the Church, shall have the right to appeal to the District Meeting."[54] The church directory containing all this disciplinary material also appeared in the *Free Christian Baptist Hand-Book* (1873).[55]

Although discipline had theoretical prominence in Free Baptist literature, an 1860 report presented to the Free Christian Baptist General Conference of New Brunswick on the state of the churches identified two primary causes of the low state of the churches: a lack both of regular and faithful ministerial work and of proper church discipline. The report

40

then called for more attention to these two areas.[56]

Church Minutes   Church minutes revealed the actual operation of discipline among Maritime Baptists. Most churches adopted disciplinary guidelines suggested by associations for stressing preventive discipline through believer's baptism and regenerate membership. The Fredericton, New Brunswick, Church agreed in 1815 that between one and three months should elapse between the time an individual "related his experience" and the time he was "taken into the church." This procedure was designed "to prevent hypocrites from creeping into the church."[57]

Basically, three levels of corrective discipline existed: admonition, suspension, and exclusion. Admonition was the initial stage of discipline and was a caution for a wayward member to amend his ways. Sometimes, admonition was given repeatedly before more stringent forms of discipline were exercised. In 1869 in the North River Church in Prince Edward Island, a member who "had forsaken the cross and leadership of Christ and still persisted in his waywardness" was excluded only "after having received two letters of admonition from the church and pastor, and two pastoral visits."[58]

Suspension was a more rigid form of discipline. A suspended member usually lost the right to share in the ordinances and to vote. Frequently, it was administered while a member's "case" was being discussed by a church. In 1810 in the Prince William and Queensbury, New Brunswick, Church, a member was suspended "until God should bring him to a sense of his duty" because he had not followed biblical guidelines in bringing a disciplinary charge against another member and because he refused to hear the admonition of the church on this matter.[59] The Onslow, Nova Scotia, Church resolved in 1867 that any member who intentionally refused to share in the Lord's Supper or contribute to the financial support of the church should be suspended from all church privileges until he made satisfactory acknowledgement. Should the person fail to make such acknowledgement after sufficient time was given, then he was to be excluded.[60]

Exclusion was the most severe form of discipline used

by churches. In exclusion a person's membership in a church was terminated by public announcement. Restoration could occur only after the former member manifested satisfactory repentance. The right of churches to exclude members was beyond question. To illustrate, in 1844 the Alexandra, Prince Edward Island, Church resolved that "the church is autonomous through divine grace to withdraw from every member who walks disorderly according to the direction given in 1 Cor. 5:11. 2 Thess, 3:6 until he comes to repentance and should he prove obstinate to exclude him from the church."[61]

After a member was excluded from the Cornwallis Church, the Clerk placed a poem about discipline in the minutes of February 12, 1820, with four verses focusing on the warning, anguish, isolation, and hope of discipline:

Dear members all a warning take
And every darling sin forsake
Our garments keep unspotted white
Make Christ the theme of our delight.

Our hearts are pained to see removed
A brother who was thus reprovd
And now his seat is vacant made
We wish he had the church obeyed.

From all our fellowship withdrawn
How solitary and forlorn
He must now wander all alone
No former brother will him own.

We hope the Lord will him direct
For his commands to have respect
And like the prodigal of old
Return to Christ's most precious fold.[62]

Although extremely heinous sins sometimes resulted in immediate exclusion, churches frequently exercised patience before proceeding to this step. According to the June, 1845, records of one church in a case against a member, "the church having borne with him for the space of upward of a year and a

42

half using means in the meantime to bring him to repentance" chose a deacon "to visit him once more to labour with him" and let him know that he would be publicly excluded if he remained obstinate.[63]

Besides giving extensions of time to alleged guilty parties before meting out discipline, churches also formed committees to visit these members. Churches frequently sent out such committees after examining membership lists and discovering delinquent members. Such an examination in the Horton Church in 1852 produced the names of forty-four persons. The church voted that the examining committee, comprised of the pastors, deacons, and other members in good standing, do "all in their power in reclaiming and bringing back delinquent members to the church of Christ from whom they have unhappily wandered."[64]

Churches restored excluded members when they sensed that repentance had taken place. On March 22, 1779, the Horton Church suspended Daniel Sanford for fornication. On May 6, 1780, the church excluded him. Of considerable interest was that the church restored Sanford to membership almost nineteen years later, on April 7, 1799.[65]

Beginning in the 1850s various comments in the minutes of the Horton Church suggest that discipline was on the decline. In 1857 the pastor stated in a letter to the church that "The discipline of the church cannot be maintained. I say it with shame: there is not moral power in the church sufficient to discipline its own members."[66] In 1862 a committee appointed to study the state of the church reported, "It is evident that the church is not in a healthy condition. Its financial, disciplinary, and aggressive operations seem to be almost paralyzed."[67] The committee believed that the church "without fear or favor" should "proceed in the work of discipline, though it should decimate our members."[68] In 1864 "The pastor spoke of the desirableness of restoring the discipline of the church and stated the experience of the past."[69] In 1870 "In consequence of a feeling expressed by some of the members that a committee of discipline was unnecessary and unusual in Baptist churches, it was resolved . . that matters of discipline be left for the future with the pastor &

deacons."[70]   This represented a definite departure from congregational involvement in discipline.

The demise of discipline appeared in the records of other churches, too. For example in an 1878 letter resigning his pastorate of the Fredericton Church, T. H. Porter lamented that "the works of the Church has come to a stand-still. We have no discipline, no systematic visitation, even of the sick and dying."[71]

Summary   Church discipline, preventive and corrective, had high priority in Maritime Baptist life in the period of this study. Associations, Free Baptist conferences, and churches dealt repeatedly with disciplinary concerns in their records. All appealed to the Bible as the basis for using discipline. Churches meted out discipline for numerous kinds of offenses. Various levels of discipline existed, and the nature of an offense determined which was used. Maritime Baptists knew the dangers in excessive and harsh discipline and regularly raised cautions about its application. The intended goals of discipline were spiritual therapy and redemption of an individual. Sometimes the goals were achieved; sometimes they were not. Disciplinary neglect and decline began to occur in the 1850s and continued gradually through the 1870s.

Conclusion

In their early years Maritime Baptists clearly used covenants and discipline to establish and maintain a regenerate church membership. More forcefully, covenants and discipline literally saturated church, associational, and Free Baptist conference life. A change, however, began to occur about the 1850s and continued through the 1870s. While covenants and discipline continued to be used in these years, they began to lose much of their impact and strength. What factors accounted for this change? A few suggestions seem in order.

To begin with, rather than write their own individual covenants, Maritime Baptists churches tended largely to adopt

44

covenants derived from sources in the United States and printed as models in Maritime association and conference minutes and in church manuals. Because individual churches failed to struggle with, think through, and write down the disciplines of their faith in personalized covenants designed to meet specific needs, they gradually found the documents to have less and less meaning, especially when they failed to revise them to meet the demands of changing times.

Further, Maritime Baptists began to develop a negative reaction to what may have seemed a fairly legalistic application of covenants and discipline. Rather than meet the pastoral needs of the people, discipline sometimes came off as a superficial effort to preserve the sanctity of the church at the expense of every member who violated even the slightest covenantal rule or expectation. Coupled with this was the apparent belief that emphasis could best be placed on preventive discipline. These same reactions to discipline occurred among many Baptists in the United States in the late nineteenth century.

Lastly, discipline in some churches moved away from its traditional role as the task of the entire congregation and was assigned to a small committee of members, frequently the pastor and deacons. Congregations as a whole no longer needed to concern themselves with disciplinary matters that previously claimed their attention. Thus, their interest in this area diminished.

The Role of the
African United Baptist Association
in the Development of
Indigenous Afro-Canadians
in Nova Scotia, 1782 to 1978*

SAVANAH E. WILLIAMS

People of African origin have been present in Nova Scotia for three centuries. Numerically they have always constituted a small percentage of the population. And, since the Canadian Census classified its population by country of origin[1] and Afro-Canadians were denied that identity once they arrived in North America, a large percentage of the Nova Scotian Afro-Canadian population is listed under the category of "Other."[2] Nevertheless, the current population is estimated

---

* The African Baptist experience in North America was first introduced to me as a child growing up in Virginia. As I grew from childhood to adulthood, I came to know the important role of the church in the religious and secular life of my community and other Afro-American communities in the United States. As a resident of Nova Scotia, Canada, I have come to the realization that the African Baptist Church here serves the same roles in the lives of many of the people who are descendants of Black Loyalists and Refugees. Historically, Canada and the United States are quite different, however, there are many parallels in the roles of the African Baptist Church in these two countries. Even though this article is not of a comparative nature, it is written with extensive exposure to the African Baptists in both countries and without membership or vested interest in the Baptist Church. This paper is an introduction to research in progress on the African United Baptist Association of Nova Scotia.

to be between 20,000 and 25,000. Although a portion of this population has come to Canada since the 1950s, largely from the Caribbean, the Afro-Canadian presence in Nova Scotia has been felt continuously since 1749 when British settlers arrived with their slaves.[3]

Despite the historical and anthropological importance of the African Baptist in Canadian society, the literature has been sparse and scattered.[4] Because the church is the oldest and the major institution in the communities of descendants of Black Loyalists and Refugees, this paper will be an overview of the role of the African Baptist Church.

This presentation will be divided into historical periods, introducing the leaders, the issues of concern and the role of the church. Because the majority of the African Baptist Churches are members of the African United Baptist Association, the Association will be used as a point of reference. The Association was established in 1854, twenty-six years before the Negro Baptists attempted to organize in the United States.[5]

The Great Awakening of Discrimination in Nova Scotia

The first written record of a person of African descent in Nova Scotia is in 1605 when Matthew Da Costa arrived with the Champlain Expedition. In 1749 when the English settled in Halifax,[6] they evidently brought slaves with them, since two years later Africans were advertised for sale in Boston:

> Just arrived from Halifax and to be sold, ten strong hearty [N]egro men, mostly tradesmen, such as caulkers, carpenters, sailmakers, and ropemakers.[7]

By 1762, the colony had recognized slavery as an acceptable institution. Even though slave laws were not written as such, they were surely implicit,[8] and citizens held African people in bondage. As in many other colonies, public officials and members of the clergy owned slaves. One clergyman wrote an extensive letter to another urging him to set his slave free.[9] In some white Baptist Churches pews were reserved for black slaves. As cases in Prince Edward Island prove, conversion to Christianity and baptism did not gain

47

freedom for the slave.[10]

Free Black Loyalists and servants had arrived to add to this population by 1783. In this group were artisans and individuals with various farming skills. The hardship suffered by these people was a result of broken promises of land and provisions. Patterns of discrimination and public policies to benefit the white population evolved. Ongoing research indicates diverse skills in this population, thereby placing them in competition with white labourers for various jobs. This competition factor may be one of the variables in analyzing why their residences are outside of the centres of white settlement.

The negative activities and attitudes toward the Black Loyalists denied them a place in Nova Scotia history until recently. The title of "United Empire Loyalists" has been reserved for whites and even today, many people in the province and country think that all "Loyalists" who came to Nova Scotia were white.

The Refugee Blacks of the War of 1812 came in search of a new life, bringing with them numerous skills. Many were able to maintain themselves and the members of their families. In spite of the harsh conditions to which they were not accustomed, they built homes, petitioned for schools and churches, used their skills to farm and find other jobs — in essence they founded Afro-Canadian communities in less than two years. They were hardworking people who were no more dependent on the Government than other immigrants. Many of today's population in Preston, Hammond's Plains, Beechville and Halifax are descendants of the Refugee Blacks.

Establishing Roots — 1782 to 1792

In 1782 David George, a Black Baptist minister from Silver Bluff, South Carolina, arrived with his family and others.[11] With the blessings and permission of the governor of the province, he traveled to Shelburne where many of the Loyalists had settled. There was a large Black population in this area. There he established a congregation that was comprised of both Blacks and whites. George's ministry in Nova Scotia lasted ten years. During this time, he was confronted by a white group when he attempted to baptize a

48

white woman.[12] Because of religious and racial antagonisms, it is difficult to know the basic nature of the attack. However, George left the area and went to New Brunswick where he again found opposition to his presence.[13] He was given permission to preach to "his" people.[14] From this reference, it appears that the preaching was to be to Black people only. Shortly thereafter, he returned to Nova Scotia where he found his church being used for secular purposes.[15]

Because of the overall conditions that Black people faced in Nova Scotia, Thomas Peters made an inquiry about the possibility of their leaving. Peters was a former slave from North Caroline and a member of the Black Pioneer Corps during the American Revolution.[16] The opportune moment to move came in 1792. The British needed settlers for the West Coast of Africa and Nova Scotia's Black settlers were not satisfied with the conditions under which they lived. On January 16, 1792, 1190 people of African descent sailed for the colony of Sierra Leone, West Africa.[17] David George was one of those who went on that long voyage. With him he carried a new religion that flourishes today, and in Nova Scotia a Baptist legacy was left with those who remained.

Religious Identity — 1792 to 1832

On May 20, 1792, four months and five days after David George and the group of 1190 departed for Africa, John Burton, a native of England, arrived in Nova Scotia. He was "licensed in England as a dissenting minister,"[18] but had been "initiated into the Episcopal Church in infancy."[19] After spending a year in Nova Scotia, he went to the United States, which was his original destination.[20] While in the United States, he was baptized and ordained as a Baptist minister. He returned to Halifax where he established the First Baptist Church, Halifax. His congregation during his first year in Nova Scotia, and after he returned from the United States, used Marchington's meeting house.[21] Marchington's meeting house had been built for the Methodists by a Mr. Marchington, but was unoccupied when Burton arrived.[22] After Burton became a Baptist, he lost Marchington as a patron.[23] In 1795, an edifice was built with contributions from the membership and sums he had collected in different parts of

49

the United States.[24] The congregation was integrated racially. The influx of Blacks to Nova Scotia after the War of 1812 added adherents to Burton's church.

When a leadership struggle took place in St. Paul's Anglican Church in Halifax in 1824, dissenters joined Burton's Church.[25] However, these dissenters were not happy in the church and eventually established their own church. They fought for the status of *First* Baptist Church of Halifax, but lost the title, which was given to Burton's church,[26] although the former eventually won the struggle.

A new member to Burton's church around 1816 was Richard Preston, a former slave from Virginia. Preston had been converted in Virginia in 1815[27] and arrived in Nova Scotia in 1816.[28] According to MacKerrow, he had come in search of his mother who had "gone to Canada, but to what place he could not tell."[29] He found her "residing at a district by his own name."[30]

Preston became active in the church and worked with the Reverends John Burton and Edward Manning. "The coloured brethren . . . and Father Burton gave him much information and assistance, that produced a great success to the cause of christianity . . . When a request was made for Preston's ordination, it was considered by some that he had not acquired sufficient knowledge of theology to be ordained. . . ."[31] As a result, Preston was sent to England in 1831 "to avoid any religious friction that might arise and to clothe him with authority to solicit aid to build a church for his brethren from the chains of sin and slavery."[32]

Ethnic Survival and Religious Growth — 1832 to 1861

One year before slavery was abolished in the British Empire, Richard Preston returned to Nova Scotia from England as an ordained Baptist minister. His credentials had come from the West London Baptist Assocation.[33] Unlike any other Baptist minister in Halifax, he had credentials from England. The theological question appeared to have been resolved, at least for those who had questioned his knowledge of theology before he left. However, as one examines the legacy which Preston left, in the Minutes of the Association and activities of today's African Baptist Churches, the question can be raised again.The theological question has been raised in the Black Baptist Churches in the United States.[34]

Shortly after Preston returned, he organized the first African Baptist Church, Cornwallis Street Baptist Church. The church was established on April 14, 1832, with branches at Dartmouth, Preston, Beech Hill, and Hammond's Plains.[35] Cornwallis Street was resolved to be the "Mother Church."[36] Even though this group of churches appeared to be an organization, the official church organization was not established until September 1, 1854.[37] The birth of the African Baptist Association came twenty-two years after Preston's ordination and forty-one years before the establishment of the National Baptist Convention, U.S.A.[38] The Association was comprised of twelve churches, three ordained ministers and three hundred and eight members.[39] However, there were African Baptist Churches that did not and have not joined the Preston Association. The only split in the Association was from 1867 to 1880. There are now three National Baptist Conventions in the United States. The pros and cons of one African United Baptist Association in Nova Scotia will be discussed in another paper.

As was traditional among African Baptist ministers, Preston was strongly involved in social issues. No less can be said of the African Baptist Churches. In 1842, Preston organized an Ango-African Mutual Improvement and Aid Association.[40] The placement of Anglo before African must have had some significance since the word "African" has a very proud usage among African Baptists in Nova Scotia. One of the committees of this organization was concerned with political action. In 1846, Preston participated in a Negro Abolition Society.[41] The activities of these organizations will be investigated in future research.

At Preston's death on July 16, 1861, there were fifteen churches, four hundred and forty-three members, four ordained ministers and nine licentiates in the Association.[42] The churches were located in the Halifax area and along the South Shore of Nova Scotia.

The Transition Period — 1861 to 1880

The Rev. James Thomas, a Welshman, succeeded

51

Preston as the pastor of the "Mother Church" (Cornwallis Street Baptist) and several other churches. Thomas lived in Preston and was the owner of a fur company in Halifax. He was married to Hannah Hubbard of Preston, a Black woman.

Thomas had traveled extensively with Preston between 1840 and 1860.[43] He was ordained in 1857 and worked as an evangelist until Preston's death in 1861.[44] From the Minutes of the African Baptist Association, Thomas appeared to be a very important minister in the Association and was well received by the majority. However, after Preston's death, Thomas became the center of much controversy in the Association.

The Association's Minutes showed that several problems arose after Preston's death. Considering that Preston had ruled from his ordination in 1832 to his death in 1861, it seems normal that conflict would arise. Even though many of the problems are not detailed, several are mentioned, including the controversy surrounding Thomas.

The first problem was over the case of the Rev. Benson Smithers of First Preston, now known as East Preston. Smithers was a prominent minister of the Association, according to the Association's Minutes. In 1867, Smithers' credentials were revoked on the grounds of "immoral conduct."[45] Smithers not only continued to preach, but succeeded in establishing his own group which published minutes under the same name as the African Baptist Association. The eleven persons who supported Smithers against charges of immorality, which were not explicitly defined, were expelled.[46] These men eventually joined Smithers' Association. Several churches also joined Smithers. The Rev. George Neal, who moved the exclusion of Smithers, eventually was expelled himself. He joined Smithers also. This Association existed separately from the Preston Association for thirteen years, 1867 to 1880.

Two years after Smithers was expelled, Thomas resigned from First Preston after "disciplined members exercised unprincipled means to impeach [him] but the plans resorted to proved a failure."[47] In the same year, 1869, Joseph Cox of Cornwallis Street Baptist Church, brought a suit against Thomas in the Supreme Court of Nova Scotia.[48] This suit was to have "Thomas removed as Trustee of the 'Mother

Church.' But it was unsuccessful and Cox was excluded from the church on the grounds that he published false and deflamatory statements regarding Thomas."[49] The conflict continued until May 27, 1872, when "a meeting took place in which . . . old foundations and a code of laws were sustained with their present pastor, Rev. Thomas."[50] In spite of this conflict being resolved, the African Baptists remained divided until after Thomas' death. Inasmuch as Smithers and Thomas appear to have been the two strongest leaders after Preston's death, leadership was probably the major focus of the conflict. At various meetings, presentations were alternated between Smithers and Thomas. Since Thomas and his son, the Rev. John Thomas, were the only white ministers in the Association and the majority of the Association membership was Black, colour was more than likely one of the variables that contributed to the split, but just one of the variables.

In spite of the difficulties of this transition, several activities should be noted. The church doctrine was presented in written form: the Article of Faith and Practice, Concerning A Visible Church of Christ and the Discipline, and the Covenant.[51] These church documents appear in the Association which supported Thomas. In 1883, a resolution was passed to unite with the Baptist Convention meeting at Moncton.[52] The following year, representatives of the Association were in attendance at the Convention.

In the midst of the conflict and declarations, Peter E. MacKerrow, Clerk of the Association, reminded the membership that "he hoped [that] the day would soon dawn when the cloud of prejudice that . . . [hangs] over the descendants of 'Africa' in [this] province particularly would soon be dispersed when we will be able to breathe a clearer atmosphere than we now do. The condition of the people of colour in the province," he said, "was deplorable, none worse throughout the Dominion, for although [their] votes are sought both in parliamental and civic elections, yet no recompense [did] they receive, but [had] to put up with the meanest of school houses that the province can afford, which deserves the greatest censure from the educated world."[53] MacKerrow wrote the first history of Afro-Canadians in Nova Scotia in 1895, *A Brief History of the Coloured Baptists of*

Growth During A Period of World Turbulence — 1880 to 1936

The Association united after Thomas's death in 1879. An influx of new ministers from the United States added to the Association's ministry from 1880 to 1936. The Reverends Wilton R. Boone and Henry H. Johnson, graduates of Newton Theological Seminary in Newton, Massachusetts, were among the first of these new ministers. By 1936, the Reverend W. A. White of Virginia had become a prominent leader in the Association. Nova Scotians such as the Reverends A. W. Jordan, Edward Dixon, A. Clements and W. N. States left their legacies.

The Rev. A. W. Jordan, a graduate of Acadia and McMaster Hall, with graduate studies at Morgan Park in Chicago, had at his death earned the title of Doctor of Divinity.[54] James R. Johnston, Clerk of the Association from 1906 to 1915, was graduated from Dalhousie Law School in 1898.[55]

The membership grew steadily from "five hundred and twenty in 1880 to six hundred and forty-eight in 1914. . . . By the end of World War I in 1920, the membership had reached seven hundred and sixty-seven and nine hundred and forty-two in 1925. . . . Even though there was a drop in membership before the Depression, there was an increase during the Depression" (1930-739; 1935-858).[56] In 1898, J. R. Johnstone, who had introduced the Baptist Young People's Union at Cornwallis Street Baptist Church, made a presentation to the Association on the establishment of Youth Unions in other churches.

By the early 1900s, the contact with African Baptists outside of the province had extended only to the United States. So when a member of the Association visited Ontario during this period, he returned to propose a relationship with the Upper Canada Association, presumably the Amherstburg Association. He felt that "the association would be productive."[57] Nevertheless, no action was taken.

A strong relationship between the church and the community continued. In preparation in 1882 for the Jubilee Year Celebration at Cornwallis Street Baptist Church, there was a desire not only to recall the glorious history of the church, but to show the community at large "what religion and education [was] doing for the race . . ."[58] Ever aware of the "corrupt and prejudice-laden atmosphere of the so-called Christian Aristocracy, who despise the poor, many of whom are made poor by their [the Christian Aristocracy] vicious legislation. . . .,"[59] the display of this progress was of great importance to the church.

Community awareness was demonstrated in the establishment of an Aid Society for the sick,[60] as well as the Normal and Industrial Institute.[61] In 1917, "Rev. M. B. Puryear of Pennsylvania, who was Moderator of the Association, introduced to the provincial government the Association's idea of the Nova Scotia Home for Coloured Children."[62] In the same year, "a cottage was found to house the Home near the Institute with Miss Julia Jackson, a teacher recruited from Philadelphia."[63] The cottage only lasted for about one month because of the great Halifax Explosion of December 6, 1917.[64] Miss Jackson returned to her home in Philadelphia.[65]

A replacement for the cottage was established four years later, after J. A. R. Kinney was hired to raise funds for a new facility. The Rev. A. A. Wyse of Cherrybrook located the McKenzie farm just outside of Cherrybrook and in 1921 the Home's gala opening took place. The complex contained a farm, living quarters for the children and adults. A school was included as a part of the Home. The Association pledged $1,000 annually, but has never fulfilled this promise. Kinney devoted most of his life to this organization which still exists today.

In spite of the fact that the Association was involved from the initial stage of the idea, it was not until 1974 that the first Black person, the Rev. Donald Fairfax, became President of the Board of the Home. Even more recently, Blacks have come to constitute the majority of the Board. In 1978, the Home moved into new facilities.

The female society which MacKerrow spoke of in 1883 was finally established in 1917.[66] The objective of the Ladies' Auxiliary was the "stimulation of the spiritual, moral, social, educational, charitable and financial work of all the local churches of the African Baptist Association. . . ."[67] Numerically and financially, the Ladies' Auxiliary is the strength and backbone of the Association. During various years, the Auxiliary has raised more money than the total receipts of the Association. As to the other objectives, further research needs to be done. Nevertheless, it appears that women's organization has been more productive than the Laymen's Council, which is composed of men. This seems to prove MacKerrow's conviction in 1883 that "their [women's] labours are generally more successful than the males."[68] In addition to the church oriented Ladies' Auxiliary, an Auxiliary, composed of many of the same women, was organized to support the programs of the Nova Scotia Home for Coloured Children. The First Congress of Coloured Women in Canada was held in Halifax in 1920.[69]

In 1919, the Association was incorporated as the African United Baptist Association with the objective to "maintain the educational, moral and spiritual welfare of the African race."[70] With various programs, the Association has continued to attempt to fulfil these objectives, sometimes under duress.

During World War I, the No.2 Construction Battalion was formed entirely of Black soldiers. The Rev. W. A. White was a captain. The Rev. M. Puryear said "the African race was making history, and when it reached the century mark, providing it holds fast to the faith, the record would be one of which it would be justly proud." Continuing his speech to the Association, he said, "the time for the Coloured Canadians to enter the struggle is now. We should fill up quickly the ranks of the No.2 Construction Battalion, for a failure on our part to comply with the request of the Government would be an insult to the Flag under whose protection we have enjoyed the fullness of freedom for over 100 years and we would also prove ourselves unfaithful as Baptists."[71] The Association placed itself on record as being "in hearty sympathy with the Empire's struggle," and pledged itself "to do all in its power to encourage coloured men to uphold the traditions of their country, and of the empire to which they belonged."[72] The No. 2 Battalion is remembered as a major contribution of Black Nova Scotia in World War I.

The Association grew from one pastor and no divinity students in 1905 to five pastors and three students by 1910. By 1936, growth in membership and churches was evident. Even the number of young Nova Scotians entering the ministry increased. At the beginning of the Depression, a five-year programme was recommended to support the activities of the church and the community.[73] The programme was initiated under the direction of the Rev. W. A. White, the Moderator of the Association. Even though the objectives of the programme were not fulfilled, goals were established during a period of crisis.

Three ministers who appeared to be very active during this period were the Reverends W. A. White, W. N. States, A. A. Wyse. An international awareness was reflected in the Association by the reporting of various topics, such as, the Boer War, the death of Queen Victoria, and the role of Black people in the world. The Association's Minutes have not indicated such an extensive view of international affairs since this period.

Shortly before the Rev. White's death on September 9, 1936, he received an honorary Doctorate of Divinity from Acadia University, his alma mater.[74] Since then, two other Black Nova Scotians have received honorary doctorate degrees. Dr. W. P. Oliver, of Lucasville, has received degrees from the University of King's College and his alma mater, Acadia. Dr. Oliver has been an active member of the Association since 1936. During the last forty years, he has held various leadership roles in the Association, the Maritime Baptist Convention, and a number of community and educational projects.

Dr. Carrie Best, of New Glasgow, has received an honorary Doctorate of Law from St. Francis Xavier University. She was the first Black woman in the Atlantic region to publish a newspaper, the *Clarion*.

Challenge and Change in a New Era — 1936 to 1978

Afro-Canadian people in Nova Scotia have survived under extremely difficult conditions. They have survived slavery, two large exoduses of many of their people to Sierra Leone, West Africa, and the United States, discrimination, the

Depression, and two world wars. In spite of all of these pressures, the Association and the communities grew spiritually, educationally, and economically.

By 1945, the influence of the work of the Education Committee of the Association had provided twenty-five graduate teachers from Normal School. Today, a number of the Association members are teachers, including one of the pastors. One minister is a vice principal of a high school.

In the early part of this period the Baptist Youth Fellowship Union organized a new Youth Convention. In addition, youth oratorical contests were held in the Association. These contests gave the youth opportunities to express their views on various issues. Several times, the winners went on to compete at the Maritime Baptist Convention.

Two changes within the Maritime Baptist Convention had an impact on the Association and on leadership in the communities which it serves. The first change prevented the licensing of ministers lacking university training in spite of the fact that laypersons in the African Association must replace the ministers at various services in order for the churches to survive spiritually. The restriction of ministers without university degrees reduced tremendously the number of licentiates who entered the ranks without formal education. The second change made an exception to the university requirement provided one "had served exceptionally for five years."[75] As of today, the records indicate that only one African Baptist Minister has met this requirement.

Other roles have changed during the last twenty-five to thirty years. The one and only woman to acquire the status of pastor in the Association was Mrs. Agnes Waring, a white missionary who served at the Second Baptist Church, New Glasgow. Three laypersons have become Moderator of the Association, a position formerly held only by ministers. Deacon R. S. Symonds of Halifax was the first, followed by Ross Kinney, also of Halifax. In 1976, Mrs. Pearleen Oliver became the first woman to hold the position. Mrs. Oliver is the author of *A Brief History of the Coloured Baptists, 1782-1953*. The publication of this book in 1953 was to celebrate the 100th Anniversary of the Association. Miss Alma Johnston, who at
58

present is the Treasurer of the Association, is the first and only woman to hold the position.

One of the most beloved women of the Association, Mrs. Muriel States, of Dartmouth, served the church and community for thirty years as the organizer of the Ladies' Auxiliary. During these many years, she traveled the province raising funds for the Association, while sharing the daily life and activities of the people she met. Mrs. States, the widow of the Rev. W. N. States, is affectionately known as the "Mother of the Association." This year, 1979, she celebrates her 91st birthday. She and Mrs. Edith Samuels Sparks, who resides in Toronto, are two of the women who were present at the establishment of the Ladies Auxiliary in 1917. These women and many more represent the strength of the African Baptist Churches even though their roles continue to be along traditional lines.

Several community and church organizations and committees that developed between 1936 and 1956 were the Nova Scotia Association for the Advancement of Coloured People, the Committee on Social Service and Child Welfare, and the Committee on Rural and Urban Life. The NSAACP was organized to undertake concerns of civil injustices. Leaders and members of the Association were active in this organization. The two committees were established to serve community needs; however, it appears that they serve to keep community issues before the Association rather than act as instruments of social change. In 1964, "the Urban and Rural Life [Committee Report] jolted our slumbering memory on the goals we [the Association] failed to reach in [the] drive for first class citizenship."[73]

By 1964, in spite of the illustrious history of the Association, and community organizations, first class citizenship had not been obtained. The small numbers and low economic status of the majority of the Black population had prevented the people from assuming full support for their churches and community programs. It is only through the help of the Home Mission Board of the United Baptist Convention that many of the churches survive. Today there are eight ministers serving the Association: William P. Oliver, Harold

59

Cornish, Donald Thomas, Donald Fairfax, Donald Skeir, William Clayton, Joseph Mack and Calvin Symonds. The average age of the first seven ministers is fifty. The Rev. Symonds was ordained less than a year ago and is the youngest member.

Since there are twenty-two churches and eight ministers, several ministers serve more than one congregation and some churches are pastorless. In one case, one minister serves three churches. The years of service for the majority of these ministers range from twenty-five to forty years. These ministers represent the only generation of Black ministers present in Nova Scotia. One young man is in seminary at present but it is not clear which denomination he will choose.

In 1957, the Baptist Youth built on the Education Committee's previous effort by establishing a scholarship fund. In the 1930s and '40s, funds were provided for educating ministers for the Association. The new fund provides general university scholarships. By 1968, five scholarships had been given and as of 1974, 124 scholarships had been awarded amounting to over $14,000.[77] These scholarships continue to be given without the recipients having to make any obligation to the Association. As a matter of fact, many recipients are young people who are not active participants in the church and quite often express the view that the church is useless.

The Association, not unlike other institutions of its kind, has not grown to the extent where it has been able to accommodate or blend the old and the new, the young and the matured. Two problems appear to have had a negative impact on the Association. First, the Association has never had a full-time paid person responsible for directing its short and long term programmes. The Moderator, who traditionally has been a minister with other responsibilities, coordinates the programmes with the assistance of chair-persons of committees. Second, the problem of obtaining new leaders appears to have grown even more serious because over the past thirty years, the Association has isolated itself by looking within the province for leaders (ministers) rather than wherever they could find them. This isolation has also reduced external exposure within North America except through the
60

limited resources of international news and regular international programs. As opportunities became available, young ministers left for Ontario or the United States. The influx of new ministers from the United States and other parts of Canada has declined sharply since the early part of the century. Attendance at national and international conferences by clergy and laypersons is very low.

In the early 1950s when new Black immigrants came to Nova Scotia, they sought out the African Baptist Church because they were Black, not because they were Baptists. Today, the population has grown to the point that places of employment and residence determine the degree of contact Black people born outside of Nova Scotia and Canada have with the African Baptist Churches and the communities they serve.

With the growth of concern for civil rights in the 1960s and '70s in the United States, there was a spillover into Nova Scotia with visits from the Black Panther Party and the Rev. Ralph Abernathy of the Southern Christian Leadership Conference. Because of historical differences, the struggle for civil rights in Nova Scotia never reached the level of social or political challenge which it did in the States. The division over ideology and methodology dispersed the potential power which could have influenced change. Blacks became divided into two groups: "Canadian" (Nova Scotian born, second to fourth generations) and "foreigners" (residents and citizens from the Caribbean and the United States). The Black United Front was established during this period as an umbrella organization for Black groups and the Human Rights Commission of the Nova Scotia Government was formed to deal with social injustices. These two organizations still exist today.

The issues of housing, education, unemployment, social injustices and land were the major problems during this period. The Association and community groups dealt with these concerns separately and in some cases simultaneously. In several cases conflict between the young and the matured, as well as the "Canadians" and "foreigners" caused serious breakdowns in progress. The inconsistencies of the

Association are best exemplified in its response to issues of controversy. Even though most people think of the African church and its community as one and the same, the Association seems to be able to separate community and church when it is not sure about the ramifications of its involvement in controversial issues.

Another separation of church and community takes place when it comes to politics. The folk religion of Blacks in Nova Scotia is used for political purposes only to obtain community resources, not to challenge political and public policies, nor to further the political careers of Blacks, at least not in an overt manner. For many, the most obvious leaders in the communities have been ministers and church officers, but none have ever run for political office beyond the local level. In a province where the oldest and largest Black communities of Canada exist, no Black has ever been elected to provincial or federal political office. However, considering Canada has only had one Black in Parliament in its history, the present Minister of Labour, Lincoln Alexander of Ontario, the phenomenon is not unique to Nova Scotian Blacks. It appears that population size and interest group pressure influence the political arena even in the country where the terminal of the underground railroad supposedly represented freedom.

When the Association has involved itself in social and community concerns, it has often failed to achieve stated objectives (for example, the financial pledge to the Nova Scotia Home for Coloured Children or the 1930 five-year programme of church and community efforts). This failure can be attributed, in part, to the lack of a strong economic and political framework within the Black community and the Association itself. In addition, the Association's intellectual growth has not been sufficiently stimulated to a point where ideas and philosophies are either re-evaluated or new ones established.

"The Blacks in Nova Scotia are poorer than the average White Nova Scotian and Nova Scotians are poorer than the average Canadian."[78] However, the economic status of Blacks in Nova Scotia is diversified just as it is in the white Nova Scotian population, in spite of the image that is presented in

62

newspaper articles and scholarly publications. There have been a few Black entrepreneurs during this century, including Peter MacKerrow, who was a furrier. Admittedly, today, there are fewer than ever.

Two conditions contribute to the lack of Black businesses: (1) the nature of covert institutional racism in the province and the country that leads Blacks in this province to think that they are an integral part of the social and economic structure, thereby not needing their own businesses; (2) the tendency of Canadians, including Blacks, to look elsewhere for conditions of discrimination that are perceived to be worse than those here in this country and this province. This comparative analysis restricts economic and political growth for those who are oppressed.

Even at the peak of Black awareness, there did not appear to be a strong thrust in the community or church for economic self-sufficienty. A marked change in the economic status of the Black population over the past twenty years has not been reflected in many of the communities in terms of the development of businesses or extensive support for the church. As a matter of fact, few members of the Association are self-employed or employed by Black-owned businesses. In considering the economic status of Black Nova Scotians, we cannot overlook the continuous emigration of many church and community persons to other parts of Canada and the United States since the turn of the century. We must also consider the exodus of 1190 to Sierra Leone in 1792 as reducing the early economic foundation of Black communities inasmuch as many of the emigrants were artisans and skilled persons.

In the "Rural and Urban Life Report" in 1971, Dr. W. P. Oliver acknowledged the extent of change that had taken place outside of the African Baptist Church. Under the category of "Who Are We Working With" in his report, he stated the following:

> It used to be said that eighty-five per cent of the Black people in Nova Scotia were Baptist. Our population was 13,000 then; today Nova Scotia has a population of

close to twenty-five thousand and we list a church membership of approximately fifteen hundred. We can no longer claim 85% of the Black population. There are hundreds of West Indians, Africans, and Americans who are not Baptist, who have never been inside one of our churches. These people are Black, they are living in Nova Scotia. Many are highly educated and hold prominent positions in our province. They are unwillingly to accept some of the things that we Nova Scotians have taken for granted, they want change. What consideration have we given to these newcomers, have we talked to them, do we understand their point of view? This new dimension will be of serious significance to the future of the African United Baptist Association. These newcomers represent a new voice coming from the Black community, they are knowledgeable and articulate. The program of the church should be broad and flexible enough to be able to utilize these new talents.[78]

The Association has not begun to deal with the concern voiced by Oliver, but it must in addition address the population of their children and grandchildren who are also unwilling to accept some of the things that older Nova Scotians have taken for granted. This population is also knowledgeable and articulate. Many are highly educated and hold prominent positions in the province.

Blacks in Nova Scotia have not all been Baptists and the present indicates that all never will be. They have been African Methodist Episcopalians, Presbyterians, Pentecostals and Anglicans. Today there is still one AME church even though the Black Presbyterian church has ceased to exist. There are Blacks who are members of the Pentecostal faith, and the visit of Black Muslims to Halifax in the mid-1970s has encouraged some young Blacks to investigate further the philosophy and practices of Islam; however, it is too early to know the impact of this development. Nevertheless, there is concern among the African Baptists as to the impact of Islam on secular organizations, some of which were initially of interest to

64

members of the Association. Many young university graduates are not attending any churches; however, young parents are participating more as their families grow.

Conclusion

The Association faces the same problems of churches everywhere regardless of colour or creed: (1) leadership; (2) membership; (3) challenges to religious practices; and (4) economics. There is no doubt that the African United Baptist Association has played a significant role in the development of the religious and secular life of Blacks in Nova Scotia. And, although it is unique in being the oldest institution controlled by Blacks, control is only one aspect in its continuation as a useful organization to the communities it serves. It must find solutions to some of the problems listed above. The resolution of the problem of leadership is crucial to its survival. Membership and economics appear to be secondary to leadership. In spite of the existence of other organizations and the lack of successful programmes in the Association, it remains the major organization for Blacks in the province of Nova Scotia. Unlike other communities in Canada and the United States, where there are other secular and religious organizations, the African United Baptist Association of Nova Scotia still serves the dual role of fulfilling religious and secular needs. The survival of the Association depends on its ability to find solutions to some of its existing problems.

Without Intervention of Prophet, Priest or King

ESTHER CLARK WRIGHT

In his prayers at morning devotions, my father very often started with thanks that we were able to approach the throne of grace without intervention of prophet, priest, or king. With the amused tolerance of the young for the foibles of the older generation, I noted the frequent repetition of the phrase, and unconsciously stored it in mind. It took me many years to realize that this was a reference to the distinctive tenet of the Baptists, the competency of the individual in religion, and that it was a very meaningful phrase for my father's forebears.

My father's Loyalist ancestor, Alexander Clark, had belonged, as had his father, grandfather, and greatgrandfather, to the church at Topanemus in Monmouth County, New Jersey. The church had been started as a Friends Meeting by George Keith, a Scot intended for the Presbyterian ministry, who had turned Quaker in 1664, and had had close relations with William Penn and Robert Barclay of Pennsylvania. At a later date, George Keith developed doctrines displeasing to the Society of Friends, and conformed to the Church of England. His church at Topanemus had remained a part of the Church of England in New Jersey during the years that three generations of Clarks grew up in the neighbourhood.

66

Just when Alexander Clark joined the Baptists I have been unable to discover. He had remained on his lot in Saint John until after the incorporation of the city, when he had been admitted freeman of the new city as carpenter and blacksmith. Then he had gone to take possession of his land at Maquapit Lake, beyond Grand Lake, and later returned to Saint John in 1805 as Master Armourer of the Ordnance. In 1803, certainly, his third son, Gershom, was still faithful to the Church of England, as the following experience shows. Gershom's wife, Sarah Sauer, was expecting her fifth child in April, 1803, and her aunt had come to care for her and their four small children. As there was no indication that Sarah's time was near, on the evening of the 14th, Gershom rowed the aunt across the lake to call on friends. When they returned, they found Sarah dead, and the body of the stillborn infant beside her. Gershom kept the bodies in an ice house for several weeks, until he could take them across Maquapit Lake, down the waterway to Grand Lake, across the foot of Grand Lake, down the Jemseg River, and across the St. John River, for burial in the graveyard of the Church of England. During the interval of waiting, he composed the verses to be engraved upon the tombstone. The Gagetown Records show that the Rector of Gagetown forgot to record the burial of Sarah Clark in May, but entered it in his register for November of that year — a few days before he performed the marriage of Gershom Clark and the brave young woman who would care for his four motherless children and bear him eight more. There is no further evidence of journeys to Gagetown Rectory, and Gershom and his second wife were buried on the farm. It is not irrelevant to note here that the circumstances of the loss of the first wife were told me by one of Gershom's granddaughters, and that one of her grandsons has rendered outstanding service under the Canadian Baptist Overseas Missionary Board in Angola and Zaire.

It is not surprising that the message of the Baptist preachers, with their stress on the competency of the individual in religion, found a ready response in the hearts of the Loyalists and PreLoyalists in the scattered settlements throughout New Brunswick. The competency of the individual in religion was

67

an extension of the lessons they had already learned, the competency of the individual in economic and social life, his ability to clear the forest, to carve a farm out of the wilderness, to provide food and shelter for his increasing family, to maintain good relations with his neighbours, so that he could help them in their hour of need and receive help from them in his hour of need. To be able, in my father's phrase, to approach the throne of grace without intervention of prophet, priest, or king, to confess and receive forgiveness, to dedicate and name the children without waiting for the infrequent visit of a distant rector, to wait upon the Lord, in kitchen or bedroom, in field or woods, and to receive help and courage for the daily task and the frequent emergency, was a comforting and satisfying assurance.

Certainly the Rev. Joseph Crandall found a ready response when he visited the settlements on the Kennebecasis, the Belleisle, Grand Lake, and the St. John River in 1800. A native of Rhode Island, he had been brought up in Chester, Nova Scotia, and after much consideration and hesitation had responded to the call to preach, and had, in 1799, been ordained as pastor of the Sackville Baptist Church. Late in January of the next year he set out on the snowshoes he had made so that he could accompany a young man who was travelling by that method. After preaching in the villages along the way, Crandall reached Norton, where he found "an old pilgrim, Brother Innis. He had been converted in the army, and was a soldier of Christ. He preached in his own house, he was a man of native talents, and had a fair education for those times." James Innis accompanied Joseph Crandall, on snowshoes, through the wilderness to the Belleisle, where Crandall found friends ready and willing to convey him to the St. John River in a sleigh, on the ice.

After preaching at Waterborough, on the south side of Grand Lake, where he made many converts, Crandall went up the St. John River to Kingsclear, and later as far as Woodstock. When he came down the river in May, he found all the lowlands flooded, and thought of going home to Sackville, but "the boats came in loaded with anxious inquirers asking about the reformation up the river, for they had heard about such numbers being immersed, that many had been lead to read their bibles, and were prepared to yield obedience to the Lord's commands." Many of these people had been members of the Congregational or New Light Church organized as the result of the visit by Henry Alline in the late 1770s. Their leader, Elijah Estabrooks, who had been absent at the time of Crandall's earlier visit, had been troubled about the omission of the baptism to which Christ called his followers, and he led the way. "Esquire Estey, an old New England Congregationalist, rooted and grounded in the old puritan practice of Infant sprinkling", also was baptized, along with Jarvis Ring, one of the founders, fourteen years later, of the church in Fredericton. Finally, Crandall went on to Saint John, with the postman, in a canoe, and their frail bark was nearly overwhelmed when they were crossing Grand Bay. After three weeks in Saint John, he returned to Sackville "by water", he reports, presumably in a schooner sailing up the Bay of Fundy.

In spite of the fact that he had been five months absent from his church, which he was pleased to find had maintained services of exhortation and conference during his absence, and from his dear wife and child, Joseph Crandall must needs go over to Nova Scotia to the meeting of the Baptist Association to request help from the brethren in organizing a church at Waterborough. In September, he returned to Waterborough in the company of Edward Manning, pastor of the Cornwallis Church, and Theodore S. Harding of the Horton Church, who had been deputed to undertake this mission. The church was duly organized, and Elijah Estabrooks was ordained as pastor. Then Crandall and Harding returned to Norton, where they organized a church and ordained Brother Innis as pastor. (James Innis, it will be remembered, was later imprisoned for a year, and fined £50, for performing the marriage ceremony for two of his parishioners in a province where only Church of England clergy were authorized to perform marriages by license.) Edward Manning went up the river to Prince William, where he had preached in 1793 and had been heartily endorsed by the Magistrate, Isaac Allen, formerly colonel of the New Jersey Volunteers, who had been sent to censor him. In

November of 1800, Manning was able to get the church in Prince William organized, but there is no record of a pastor being ordained for that church.

All of this emphasizes an important point. Little has been said in the histories of the Baptist denomination in the Maritimes of the work of the laymen in maintaining the Baptist churches. During the five months that Joseph Crandall was absent in the western part of the province, again when he was attending the Association in Nova Scotia, and again when he was helping with the organizations of the churches at Waterborough and Norton, the services of the church at Sackville were carried on by the deacons and the lay members of the church. Edward Manning was absent from Cornwallis for at least three months in 1800, and Theodore Harding from Horton for a shorter period. The church at Horton apparently had carried on from 1791, when Nicholas Pierson, the shoemaker who had been ordained as pastor, left for Hopewell, New Brunswick, until 1795, when T.S. Harding began his long pastorate. Edward Manning, writing in 1838 about the work on the St. John River, said there were Baptist Churches in many places and no stated minister. With only occasional help from itinerant preachers and the pastors of the larger churches, the faithful members kept the Sunday services, sometimes the Sunday Schools, and often the weekly conference meetings going. Apparently that state of things continued until late in the nineteenth century: the competency of the individual in religion made it possible to carry on without prophet, priest, or king — or even an ordained Baptist minister.

Histories of churches, obituaries of faithful members, personal recollections, provide a few glimpses of how the work went on. Henry Steeves, the fifth son of one of the pioneer settlers on the Petitcodiac River, is supposed to have started a church in Hillsborough about 1795, and to have kept on preaching until 1822 or thereabouts. His older brother, Christian, one of the two brothers to receive their portion of their father's land above Moncton, moved further up the Petitcodiac to take advantage of the bounty the province offered to those who would settle in remote areas and provide

70

shelter for travellers, and there he preached in the settlements in the surrounding country. His grandsons and greatgrandsons, some as lay preachers, continued the work. The story is told of one greatgrandson who was accustomed to wrestle mightily and at such length in prayer at morning devotions, that his wife knelt at a chair near the door so that she could slip out and feed the chickens!

Christian Steeves' eldest daughter, Rachel, married Robert Colpitts, second son of the Robert Colpitts from County Durham, England, who had come out with the Yorkshire settlers in the 1770s, but on going back for wife and family had been unable to return to New Brunswick until after the close of the Revolutionary War. The second Robert Colpitts, after the death of his eldest son at the age of seven, became deeply concerned about religion, and began to preach. After "toiling hard through the week with his hands for the support of his family," *The Religious Intelligencer* reported in his obituary in November 1855, "it was no uncommon thing for him on a Saturday night, when the tide served, to row his boat several miles to attend an appointment the next day, and return the following night. He resided at this time about four miles below the Bend of the Petitcodiac (i.e., Moncton) and frequent were his visits to Hillsborough on the opposite side of the river...as also to Shepody." Later, Robert Colpitts moved to Dutch Valley, near Sussex, then to Upper Sussex, and later to Dickie Mountain, north of Norton. For about forty-eight years he continued preaching, but it was not until he was past sixty that he, and at the same time his son-in-law, Edward Weyman, were ordained by Elders Hartt and Cronkhite of the Free Baptist Association.

Minutes of the churches show them struggling along with very little help from outside. When the Baptist Association met at Waterborough, as it did several times, the ministers would take advantage of the opportunity to visit in the communities round about and conduct preaching missions. Eventually, a church was organized at Canning, across Grand Lake, in the area where Gershom Clark had lived. In 1850, the Canning Baptists were able to erect a building for worship, and by renting out the pews they had nearly enough to pay the £25 for Elder Miles' services for a quarter of his time. The collections, which varied from one shilling to one pound a week, helped with these and other expenses. Groups at Scotchtown and at Douglas Harbour also secured their quarters of Elder Miles' services. In 1856, when the Rev. Isaiah Wallace visited the area on behalf of the Home Missionary Society, a church was organized at Scotchtown, and the Society agreed to allow him to remain for several months in the area. Later, there is mention of Elder Strang, who preached at intervals and baptized several who had related their Christian experience at conference meetings. In 1867, a Sunday School was begun. On May 9, 1869, the Scotchtown Church "resolved to engage Rev. Gilbert Springer to preach half of the time for six months which resulted in nothing very special." They did admit that the congregations had generally been very large, but the conference meetings had remained small and poorly attended. After that, nothing more was recorded until 1884, by which time the church building was in a bad state and meetings were held in the homes until repairs were effected.

In the 1830s, there was a young storekeeper in Fredericton who had evidently taken a leading part in the work of the church, for he answered a call from Charlotte County for help in the Baptist work there. Richard Burpee became the first New Brunswicker to graduate from Acadia College, and the first Protestant foreign missionary from British North America. Fifty years later, another storekeeper in Fredericton walked every Sunday afternoon the three miles to Nashwaaksis to conduct a Sunday School there. In spite of the demands of an increasingly large business, in spite of ten years as Mayor of Fredericton during the difficult years of the depression, followed by five years as Member of Parliament, and five years as Lieutenant Governor of New Brunswick, W. G. Clark continued to serve the Brunswick St. Baptist Church, for many years as teacher in the Sunday School, then as Superintendent, as member of various boards, as deacon, as promoter and generous contributor for church projects, faithful attendant at Sunday and midweek services, frequent delegate to Convention and representative on various boards.

It is a good thing to give recognition to the Crandalls, the Mannings, the Hardings, for their pioneering work, for their preaching missions, their baptizing of converts and organizing of the early churches, as the Baptist historians have done, but there should be recognition, too, of the laymen, who year in and year out, kept the work of the church going, who built the church edifices and maintained them, who taught in the Sunday Schools, who served as deacons and members of boards, who reached out to groups and communities outside, and helped to maintain services there.

If little has been said about the work of the laymen, still less has been said about the contribution of the women to the establishment and on going work of the churches. It was on the women that the work of entertaining the missionaries and visiting preachers fell, and it was the women who had to prepare their homes for the services held there in early times and to clean up after the incursion of the people who had tramped or driven over muddy roads. In New Brunswick, for instance, by 1800, the Loyalists had been settled for less than seventeen years, most of the Pre-Loyalists twice as long. The primitive shelters of the first years had for the most part been replaced by one-and-a-half or two storey frame houses. The kitchen, with its big fireplace, was the principal living room. There might be a parlour, seldom used, except for very special occasions, and usually shut up the winter through. Off the kitchen would be the "borning" room, where the parents slept until such time as it was needed for the mother and the newborn babe. Probably the parents would turn over this room to the visiting preacher, and climb upstairs to bunk with the children. The upstairs was often little more than a loft, with a partition or two, and wide shelves on which straw ticks were placed for beds. A fortunate visitor might find a bedstead, with slats or ropes supporting a straw tick and a feather bed, and the best of the blankets the housewife had recently woven on her loom. The housewife would bring out the best of everything the household afforded, vegetables and preserves from the cellar, meat from the icehouse or from the barrels of brine. From my own brief experience of home mission work sixty years ago, I recall a lad coming from the fields and remarking

73

when he saw the wild strawberry preserves on the table, "Guess the minister is coming to tea."

Nor were the women only the Marthas, careful and troubled about many things: they were also the Marys, listening attentively to the messages of the visiting preachers, giving their testimony in meetings, following, or often going before, their husbands in baptism. It was Rachel, the mother of the seven Steeves sons, who tackled William Black, the founder of Methodism in the Maritimes, about certain of his doctrines and accused him of leading her family astray. Her youngest granddaughter Mary Gross, who had always entertained visiting preachers, both before and after her husband's death, had been the first girl from Hillsborough to go away to boarding school and took seriously her responsibility to watch over the preacher's message. Mary's granddaughter, coming in from school, would find her grandmother, glasses pushed up on top of her head, the open Bible beside her, busy preparing the vegetables for dinner, and the young scholar would be asked to read aloud certain passages which Mary wished to bring to the attention of the preacher whose sermons had seemed to her to contain strange doctrines.

Joseph Crandall did mention in his Journal that he had been kindly treated everywhere, and he paid special tribute to one of his hostesses, Mrs. Case. The Cases were Loyalists from Rhode Island, and Mrs. Case was the only immersed person he had found west of Salisbury. "This dear sister received me joyfully and arose after the sermon and bore witness to the truth of the Gospel. She contributed to my support and caused others to do so as well." It is just the sort of thing the women have been doing ever since. The Baptist Churches of New Brunswick and elsewhere owe a great deal to Waitie Hopkins Case and the thousands of other women like her.

Thus, although the ministerial leadership of the early Baptist "Fathers" was crucial for the growth of the denomination, so too were the dedication and perseverance of the thousands of lay men and women who had learned to approach their God "without intervention of prophet, priest or king."

"Joseph Howe is their Devil": Controversies among Regular Baptists in Halifax, 1827-1868

PHILIP G. A. ALLWOOD

Nineteenth century Regular Baptists in North America were Calvinist and practiced close communion while the Free Baptists were Arminian and followed open communion.[1] By 1827 the Regular Baptists in Nova Scotia had established a unity in conformity. The earliest Baptist Churches in the province had been a blend of Regular, Free Baptist and Congregationalist practices. In 1809 the Baptist Association, which had been organized in 1800, declared itself to be Regular Baptist. The Free Baptists in the province would have a separate development of denominational identity.[2]

When the Baptist Association became Regular Baptist, the First Baptist Church, Halifax,[3] commonly known as John Burton's Church, joined the Association. This church had been the lone consistently Regular Baptist Church in the province. It had refused to join the Association until the non-Regular Baptists had been expelled.

Burton, an Anglican priest, had come to Nova Scotia liscenced as a Dissenting Minister from Lady Huntingdon's Society. During a trip to Knowlton, New Jersey, in 1793, he had been converted to Regular Baptist beliefs and was baptized and reordained. He returned to Halifax in 1794 and founded a Regular Baptist Church in 1795.

Burton's Church was typical of the times. Its membership was comprised largely of lower class people who were lacking in formal education. It differed from the rest of the Association by drawing heavily from the Black population of Halifax, Hammond's Plains, and Preston.[4] In 1827 this church had a membership of 280.[5]

Unity among the Regular Baptists was maintained by their adherence to a revised form of the Philadelphia Confession of Faith and, more importantly, by their lower class status. This bred a comfortable familiarity. Their leaders were largely self educated. By the late 1820's the Regular Baptists were ready to expand their witness by founding educational institutions. Unfortunately the economic and social status of the denomination prevented them from doing it.[6]

In the last half of the 1820's this would change. Over a period of forty years the unity in conformity would change to a unity in diversity.[7] In 1827 a group of upper class dissenters would enter the denomination. The conflicts in the church which they founded in Halifax serve to illustrate the changes which took place among the Regular Baptists.

Included in this group was J.W. Johnston, who would become Premier of Nova Scotia, Dr. Lewis Johnston, J. W.'s brother, E.A. Crawley, who would become a Baptist minister and an educational leader, J.W. Nutting, the prothonotary of the Supreme Court, John Ferguson, a prominent Halifax manufacturer, who would co-edit Baptist periodicals with Nutting, and John Pryor, who was also destined for the ministry and educational leadership. Unsung heros in this group were women from prominent Halifax families.[8]

In the second and third decades of the nineteenth century, the Methodist and Simeon Revivals made their impact felt in Nova Scotia. St. Paul's Anglican Church, Halifax, was influenced by this evangelical revival. When the rectorship of the church became vacant in 1824, the congregation wanted the curate, the Reverend J.T. Twining, appointed because of his evangelical sympathies. He was not supported by the former rector, the Reverend John Inglis, who had been appointed Bishop of Nova Scotia. During the two years of conflict among the ecclesiastical authorities, the congregation, and the government, congregational autonomy was one of the main issues. Eventually the congregation lost its case.[9]

A schism resulted and efforts were made to found an independent Episcopal chapel, but they failed. Some of the dissenters accepted the verdict and returned to St. Paul's Church. Others did not and organized the St. George's parish. A group of about twenty continued the independent efforts by attempting to found an independent evangelical chapel in the town. They took over the construction of a stone chapel on Granville Street which had been abandoned when the independent Episcopal efforts ceased.[10]

The group of independents had long been on friendly terms with John Burton and other Baptist ministers.[11] John Ferguson was married to the niece of Edward Manning, one of the leading Baptist ministers in the Maritime region. When looking for a Church with which to worship until the chapel was finished and a minister had been secured, the independents decided to attend Burton's Church.[12] In spite of the obvious class differences, the seceders became an integral part of Burton's fellowship.[13] This is illustrated by their attendance at the 1826 Nova Scotia Association meetings with Burton.[14]

During the course of a year with Burton, many of the group became convinced of Regular Baptist beliefs. Enough converted so that the chapel of Granville Street was opened as a Regular Baptist Church on September 30, 1827. The Reverend Ira Chase from Newton Baptist Theological Institute came to Halifax to organize the church. He brought with him Alexis Caswell, who was ordained as the first pastor of the church on October 7.[15]

The effect upon the Nova Scotia Regular Baptists was immediate. Partially as a result of the influence of these "new" Baptists, a prospectus for a Baptist Academy was drafted and accepted at the 1828 meeting of the Nova Scotia Association.[16] Unfortunately the impact of this new group upon the Halifax Regular Baptists led to the destruction of John Burton's Church.

Problems had initially occurred in the early 1820's when Richard Creed had come to Halifax as the Clerk of Works. He worshipped with the Regular Baptists but held opinions on conditional immortality and the Second Advent which brought him into conflict with them.[17] He also possessed a non-Regular Baptist doctrine of church. He received support for his attitudes from Alexander Crawford, a Scotch Baptist Elder.[18]

After creating turmoil in the Halifax Church following his arrival, a reconciliation between Creed and Burton was arranged by the Reverend Robert Davis.[19] This did not stop Creed's agitation in the congregation for he is described as a lawless Baptist in January 1827.[20]

Davis, a Welshman, had been assisting the Reverend Harris Harding in Yarmouth and conducting missionary tours in Nova Scotia for the Association. In 1827 he moved to Halifax to assist the aging Burton. He appears to have been an orthodox Regular Baptist, except for strong anti-Anglican and anti-formal education prejudices.[21]

Burton had supported the efforts to found a new church because he saw it as the means of attracting the upper class to the Baptist cause. Therefore he agreed with plans which would have seen his church dissolved. The new Granville Street Church would serve the town and churches would be founded in Hammond's Plains and Preston. Most of the Black Baptists came from the last two areas. Funds raised from selling the Old Meeting House on the southeast corner of Barrington and Buckingham Streets were to be used for support of the new rural churches.

Burton thought that he had the agreement of his church for this arrangement. But on September 30, 1827, when the new church was opened, about two hundred of Burton's congregation refused to attend the evening service at the Granville Street Chapel. Instead they conducted their own worship service.[22]

Davis, supported by Creed, led the Blacks of Burton's Church in refusing to carry out the initial plans. He objected to the educated status of the Granville Street Church founders and to the leadership given in the church by some of the

78

Anglican seceders who were really still Anglicans. Davis was able to take advantage of Black fears in furthering his opposition.

The Black Baptist misgivings were justified. Until objections had been raised, there had been a plan to use funds raised from the sale of the Old Meeting House to support the new chapel.[23] Also, Burton had been assisted by Black preachers. The leaders of the Granville Street Church would not have given any authority to these men as the "new" Baptists had even ignored the white ministers in the Maritimes and had looked to New England for pastoral leadership. The Blacks would have lost their identity in the new church.[24]

The Black Baptists would also have been irritated by the prejudices expressed against their church when the white seceders started attending the Old Meeting House. T.C. Haliburton is alleged to have represented the minister "...as charging the brethern in the gallery to spit over their shoulders today, for there were white gentlemen sitting below them."[25]

Davis maintained a worshipping congregation and claimed that it was the First Baptist Church, Halifax. Burton was surprised at the attitude of his congregation but accepted it and said that he would continue his church.[26] Thus two churches claimed to be First Baptist Church, Halifax.

The calling of an Association Council to resolve the debate illustrates the unity in conformity of the Nova Scotia Regular Baptists. The Reverends Edward Manning, Joseph Dimock, and James Munro failed as an initial council because Davis refused to co-operate.[27] But after Davis agitated against the Granville Street Church at the 1828 Association meetings, another council was formed. This one ruled in Burton's favour; Davis left town.[28]

This did not spell the end of problems for Burton. His failing health prevented him from effecting a proper reconciliation with his parishioners. By the time of his death in 1838, First Baptist Church, Halifax, had lost visibility.[29] Churches were finally organized in Hammond's Plains and Preston in 1841.[30]

Burton's failure was due also to the fact that the Black Regular Baptists were tired of the treatment which they had received from the white Regular Baptists. Some of the Halifax Regular Baptists clearly held anti-Black prejudices.[31]

The Black Baptists had come of age. When the Reverend David George and other Black leaders had gone to Sierra Leone in 1792, the remaining Black population had been left largely leaderless. By 1827 the Black Baptists had once again developed an indigenous hierarchy, foremost of whom was the Reverend Richard Preston.

After the Halifax controversy many of the Blacks continued to worship together. In 1832 the African Baptist Church was formed in Halifax with Richard Preston as the minister. Because the Blacks were considered to be under discipline by Burton's Church, this new church was refused admission to the Association.[32] The church continued its separate existence and became the mother church of the African Baptist Association.[33]

The problems caused by Davis illustrate the search for a new direction by the Regular Baptists. Davis represents the pre-1827 Regular Baptists. He had no formal education and was from the lower classes. The rejection of his views gives evidence of the desire of the Regular Baptists to broaden their denominational horizons.

The unity in conformity was shown by the acceptance of the council decision. Having lost support, Davis left Halifax. The failure of the African Baptist Church to accept authority meant that a separate denomination would be formed.

Richard Creed and his supporters became part of the Granville Street Church congregation after Davis left town. He was repeatedly refused admission to the church, but his followers, including his son George, were accepted. It is the addition of Davis' white followers which caused the rapid growth of the Granville Street Church in its first two years.[34]

At this time the Disciples of Christ denomination was developing in the United States. It would be officially formed in 1832 by the union of the "Christian" movements led by Alexander Campbell and Barton Stone.[35] The Disciples differed from the Regular Baptists by belief in baptismal regeneration, weekly observance of the Lord's Supper, and
80

open communion.[36]

The development of the Disciples of Christ denomination in the Maritimes is generally attributed to the work of Alexander Crawford. He fellowshipped with the Regular Baptists but never joined them because he was a Scotch Baptist.[37] Scotch Baptists recognized a plurality of elders from the congregation and had weekly observance of communion.[38]

One other influence in Maritime Disciple development is to be found in the Creed party in Halifax. As Campbell caused problems for the Regular Baptists in the United States, Creed created them for the Halifax Regular Baptists.

When one reads the list of names of Creed's supporters, one sees the names of Halifax families which were part of the Sandemanian Church in Halifax in the early 1800's.[39] Scotch Baptists have been described as immersing Sandemanians.[40]

In an 1827 letter, Crawford recommended to Creed that he enlist the aid of Doctor Lewis Johnston. Johnston did ally himself with Creed. He adopted Campbellite views and would edit the *Gleaner,* a Halifax Campbellite paper, in the 1830's.[41]

Thus in the Granville Street Church there was a group of people holding Sandemanian, Scotch Baptist, and Campbellite views. At the same time, many of the strong Regular Baptists were leaving the church. John Pryor and Edmund Crawley had gone to New England to study for the ministry. Caswell had resigned as pastor of the church in July 1828 to teach at Brown College. Richard McLearn, pastor of the Rawdon Baptist Church, had been in town studying with Caswell, but had left town when Caswell departed.[42]

In September 1828, the Reverend Henry Green of Andover Seminary became interim pastor. At first, he was well received. But he supported Creed's admission to the church, and thus alienated Nutting and Ferguson. They were the remaining male founders of the church. Others of the Anglican seceders were part of the church congregation but had not become members. Therefore, they had no voice in the church affairs.

By August 1829, the church was divided. Nutting and Ferguson led the minority group, made up mostly of the converted Anglicans. They wanted Crawley to return as pastor of the church. Creed and Lewis Johnston supported Green and directed the Disciple-leaning faction.

Finally, the converted Anglicans used their power as owners of the Granville Street Chapel to expel the congregation, which assumed the designation Second Baptist Church.[43] It took a council from the Association to achieve the dismission of the Nutting/Ferguson group to form a new church in the chapel, as Third Baptist Church, Granville Street. They adhered to the Covenant and Articles of Doctrine adopted in 1827, while Second Baptist abandoned them.[44]

The Second Baptist Church met in the Acadia School. It was not long before Green had to leave because his Fullerite views conflicted with the Calvinism of the church.[45]

Second Baptist Church maintained its membership in the Regular Baptist Association until 1836. During the 1830-1836 period, they had slowly accepted Disciple practices and had agitated for their adoption by the Association.[46] When the Association refused to change, the church discontinued its relationship with it. In 1837 Campbellite missionaries visited the Church.[47] By 1841 the church was known as the "Church of Christ in Halifax."[48]

Visibility of the congregation was lost in 1842. Many of its members returned to the Granville Street Chapel. Both Creed and Johnston rejoined the Regular Baptists. Part of the congregation preserved some sort of church community. This group would provide the foundation upon which the Disciples of Christ Church in Halifax would be founded in 1847.[49]

The Regular Baptist Association was changing to a postion of unity in diversity. When the Second Baptist Church urged the adoption of its policy as the standard for the Association, that body informed the church that, although its views were clearly wrong, Christian forebearance would allow the Association to continue the existing fellowship[50] The Association was willing to entertain some diversity in its midst, but the recognition of the 1830 Council's authority shows that conformity was still the basis of unity.

The decade after the above troubles was peaceful for the Halifax Regular Baptists. Some minor irritation occurred due

82

to the Reverend William Jackson's Independent Baptist Church. He was a converted Methodist Protestant. He "strained the nerves"[51] of the churches in Halifax from 1832 until about 1838.[52] In September 1834 six members of the Granville Street Church were dismissed to organize a church in Dartmouth,[53] but this was a peaceful break.

A serious challenge to Regular Baptist polity came about when the Reverend Joseph Belcher became pastor of the Granville Street Church in November 1844. Regular Baptist practice in Britain was different from that in North America and Belcher, reflecting his British Baptist background, challenged the practices of the Nova Scotia Regular Baptists.

Although the polity issue illustrates the development of the Regular Baptists, the reason given for Belcher's dismissal from the pulpit, "want of adaptation in ministry,"[54] adequately describes the personality problem he had. Belcher's grandiosity was the major cause of tension. He considered himself to be the John Knox of Halifax.[55]

Nova Scotia Baptist feelings toward the British Regular Baptists had been soured after John Pryor's tour of England in 1844 to raise funds for Acadia College, which had been founded in 1838. He had hoped to raise two to three thousand pounds, but received only eight hundred.[56] The British Baptists believed in total separation of church and state. Therefore, they did not like the government grant which Acadia received. Nor did the British Baptists sympathize with the Nova Scotia Regular Baptists' "struggles with Howe."[57]

Many members of the Granville Street Church were involved in politics; J.W. Johnston was the Attorney-General. Originally there had been a close working relationship between the political people of the church and Joseph Howe.[58] His opposition to the continuation of public funding for Acadia College had driven a wedge between them. To Howe Acadia was simply another sectarian college, of which there were already too many.[59] Animosity increased when Howe accused Ferguson and Nutting, the editors of the *Christian Messenger*,[60] of dishonesty regarding payment of the paper's printing cost.[61]

The anti-Howe feeling became so great that a New Brunswick Regular Baptist described the Nova Scotia Regular Baptists as exhibiting the Attorney-General for their God and Joseph Howe as their devil.[62]

John Pryor had also been upset at the open communion practices of the British Regular Baptists and their close working relationship with the Roman Catholics. He communicated his displeasure about his trip to the ministers and leaders of the Association.[63]

Into this animosity came Belcher, advocating changes in the Nova Scotia Regular Baptist church polity. He recommended the cessation of use of government funds for the support of Acadia. He wanted detailed financial reports. He suggested registry of births and marriages. And he wanted the Association to publish the works of the founders of the British Baptists.

This agitation did not please the leadership of the Granville Street Church, who were also leaders of the Association. A catalytic last straw came when Belcher's son went to work for Joseph Howe as a printer. Belcher was dismissed from the pastorate in August 1845.[64]

Belcher stayed in Halifax and started an independent church built around a core of the younger Granville Street members. They applied for dismission from their church but were refused and officially viewed to be in need of discipline.[65]

Belcher declared that, based on British practice, they were justified in seceding from the Granville Street Church.[66] They started building the Salem Chapel on Argyle Street. But the work collapsed when Belcher appeared in the pulpit in the vestments of an Episcopal bishop, thereby losing his congregation's support. He left Halifax in the fall of 1846.[65]

Belcher did manage to have the Association stop using government funds for Acadia by writing a letter against the Nova Scotia Baptists to a British newspaper, the *Banner,* in 1850. He criticized their failure to practice separation of church and state. The Maritime Baptists thereupon decided to use the funds solely for the support of Horton Academy.[68]

The controversy pointed out to the Association the diversity that was possible in the Regular Baptist denomination. Although Belcher's grandiosity likely prevented the Nova Scotia Regular Baptists from looking objectively at the questions he raised, the conflict would demonstrate the potential for diversity, especially as more British ministers came to serve in the Maritimes.

Another dismission, this one peaceful, took place when thirteen members of the Granville Street Church were dismissed on January 14, 1848, to form a church in the north-end of Halifax.[69]

A minor disruption occurred in 1848 when a preacher named Dealtry came to Halifax. He introduced the doctrines of sleep of the soul and annihilation of the wicked. Fifteen to twenty members of the Granville Street Church left it to join his congregation.[70] This may have been the introduction of the Adventist movement in Halifax.

The previous series of disruptions have shown how Regular Baptist polity had developed from a unity in conformity in 1827 to an incipient unity in diversity. Council authority is the sign of unity in conformity. It was the upholding of a council decision that forced the separate development of the African Baptist Association. A council had resolved the differences between the Creed/Johnston and Nutting/Ferguson parties in 1830.

At the same time, possibilities of diversity were introduced by the forbearance which the Association would have had for the Second Baptist Church and by the confrontation with the British Regular Baptist practices. But it would only be with the denial of council authority that diversity would be possible.

This would occur in 1867 when the verdict of a council, which cleared the Reverend John Pryor of charges brought against him by the Granville Street Church, was ignored. Pryor had become pastor of the church in 1862 . On the night of April 24, 1867, he was seen leaving the room of a woman of ill-repute at 2:00 a.m. He would claim that he had been making a pastoral call. The town chose to believe otherwise.

Pryor was immediately stripped of his office, as his

credibility had been destroyed. Charges were also brought agianst him by a Miss Vaas who claimed that he had deliberately falsified, for his personal profit, the accounts which he had held in trust for her. Because he could not explain, to the church examiners' satisfaction, the irregularities in the accounts, he was excommunicated from the church.[71]

Pryor appealed to the Central Association,[72] which recommended the calling of a council.[73] After much debate about its constituency, a council of ten ministers and laymen from Nova Scotia and New Brunswick met in late August 1867.

The council decision was that Pryor had been indiscreet in his pastoral visiting and unwise in handling the Vaas accounts. It also stated that the Granville Street Church should have called for a council earlier in the course of events. The church was asked to reconsider the dismissal from the pulpit and the excommunication of Pryor.[74]

The Granville Street Church refused to accept the recommendation of the council, which they saw as being for advice only.[75] This started a debate about council authority between the *Christian Messenger,* the Nova Scotia Baptist paper, and the *Christian Visitor*, the New Brunswick Baptist paper. The Reverend I.E. Bill, who had been a member of the council, was the editor of the *Visitor* and Stephen Seldon, a deacon in the Granville Street Church, edited the *Messenger.* The contending forces soon ceased arguing the question of Pryor's guilt or innocence and debated the issue of denominational authority in the convening of councils. The debate expanded beyond Bill and Seldon and raged for a year. John Payzant[76] even went so far as to produce a pamphlet advocating Episcopal government among Baptists.[77]

The debate climaxed at the Central Association's meeting in June 1868. A resolution was moved and defeated which would have made the decisions of a council, which had been called by a church for advice, binding upon the church.[79] The authority of the local church to ignore council decisions was affirmed.

Thus unity in diversity was enunciated. The Central

Association's decision allowed diversity in standards of discipline of members. Council authority would be needed to maintain a conformity in practice. As the principle came to be applied to theological and polity issues, denominational diversity would be possible among the Regular Baptists. This would open the doors to fellowship with the Free Baptists and lead eventually to the union of the Regular and Free Baptists in 1905 and 1906.

In forty years the nature of the unity of a denomination had changed. Unity is easy to maintain with conformity because one can define what one is or is not. Unity in diversity is a much more difficult state of existence. It calls for new definitions of identity. The failure of Atlantic Baptists to seek these definitions explains the tensions which have existed in the denomination ever since. The identity issue, left unresolved in 1868, still plagues the Baptists of Atlantic Canada today.

The Maritime Baptists
and Higher Education
in the Early Nineteenth Century

BARRY M. MOODY

The founding of Queen's (now Acadia) College in 1838 was an outward manifestation of inward changes that had been taking place within the Baptist community during the past generation. The road from the rabid anti-intellectualism of the late eighteenth century to the formal ministerial training of the 1840s was a long and far from easy one. Nor were all of the battles won with the establishment of the three institutions of learning operated by the Baptists by this time. However, the Regular Baptists of the Maritimes had nonetheless undergone a remarkable transformation.

The New England settlers who had come to the Maritimes in 1760 and thereafter were, in general, Congregationalists, who were in no way unfamiliar with general education. In fact, the Congregational Church traditionally had placed much emphasis on an educated clergy speaking to a well-informed audience. The excesses of the Great Awakening in New England, 1739-1744, and the move to the frontier region of Nova Scotia in 1760 had combined to weaken somewhat these traditions. In Nova Scotia, from 1760 to 1775, the Congregational Church underwent further disintegration, as the new Nova Scotians attempted to cope with crop failures, isolation, an oppressive Halifax oligarchy and economic depression. By the time of the outbreak of the American Revolution in 1775, most Nova Scotians had erratic ministerial leadership and practically no access to educational facilities of any kind. The ideals of a general education and a trained clergy were slowly eroded.

The Great Awakening in Nova Scotia, led by the charismatic Henry Alline, did much to hasten the disintegration of the Congregational Church and to erode further certain New England traditions. Although Alline had been denied any extensive formal training, he was by no means an uneducated man, using the term in its broader meaning.[1] He had read extensively if erratically, especially from the works of English divines. The theology that he taught and the movement that he led, however, were grounded much more in experience than in learning. As a critical nineteenth century observer wrote: "He himself was converted in a rapture; and ever after he sought to live in a rapture . . . ."[2] He did not attack learning or education *per se,* but he did warn that human learning substituted for divine assistance and heavenly authority aided substantially the cause of Anti-Christ.[3] Alline wrote that "I must acknowledge it appears to me very needless to be at too much pains in pursuit" of education, merely "to attain the name of a collegian." Christ after all had not said, "colleges, universities, bishops, priests, or presbyteries are the way or the door but he saith I am the way and I am the door."[4] Building on such statements, his followers, spurred by circumstances, would conceive of an uneducated clergy as not only necessary but desirable. Anti-intellectualism — a profound suspicion of learning — became a common attribute of the New Light Congregational-Baptist churches that sprang up in the aftermath of the Great Awakening.

The men who would lead the emerging Baptist movement in this formative period, 1790-1820, were, almost without exception, men of no formal training at all. Harris Harding, Edward and James Manning, Theodore Seth Harding, John Burton, Joseph Dimock, Thomas Handley Chipman and others, had come to Baptist convictions and the ministerial occupation from other faiths and by often circuitous routes. None possessed formal training in Baptist doctrine and practice; in fact, most had little institutional education of any sort.

However, it is clear from the extant diaries and letters of this period that these were not necessarily the unlettered, ignorant men often painted by their detractors, both then and since. Many of these men read very extensively, both theological and secular works, continually attempting to improve their minds. In 1814, Edward Manning confided to his diary that he had just finished reading Increase Mather's book on comets and was very impressed with it.[5] He expressed an interest in similar topics throughout his life. Charles Tupper, ordained in 1816, had behind him a total of twelve weeks of formal schooling, yet over the next twenty years taught himself a reading knowledge of at least ten foreign languages.[6] Harris Harding could write in his old age that "I would not, for mines of wealth, give up my acquaintance with Bunyan and Baxter, with Watts and Doddridge, and many, many others of like spirit. . . ."[7] Many of the ministers of the Baptist church, then, while lacking the advantages of institutional training, scarcely deserve the adjective "uneducated." Nor, it is clear, were they themselves afraid of learning, provided always that it was properly used; that is, for the greater glory of God.

The lack of formal training often proved a serious limiting factor on the usefulness of many of these early ministers. The involvement of Harris Harding, the Mannings and others in the New Dispensation movement of the 1790s, Theodore Seth Harding's temporary defection to the Masons and the Presbyterians in the second decade of the 19th century, the confusion over the relative merits of close vs. open communion — all of these problems, and many more, plagued the early "Fathers," partly at least, because their training lacked both uniformity and depth. As the result of heavy reliance on divine inspiration, and with a strong aversion to notes or a prepared manuscript, the sermons delivered often caused confusion and division. Faced with at least four hours of preaching on the following day, Saturday evening usually found Edward Manning still undecided on even the Biblical

90

text. He could only pray "O Lord, water my soul with the dews of thy grace."[8]   It is clear that the dew was not always forthcoming.

Manning, himself, recognized the dangers inherent in this less than formal approach to preaching. However, it was only in the privacy of his diary that he dared confess that

> . . . I find Sermons not Studied [i.e. prepared] (unless where God immediately calls to some sudden duty) are generally verry incoherent, and many times destitute of what ever ought to addorn a Gospel Sermon, namely, a Gospel consistency, and addresses to the Passions in Such Sermons are generally Substituted for informing the Judgment.[9]

On another occasion he recorded that "If I plow in the study, I shall reap in the Pulpit."[10] In spite of such feelings, it was not until 1821 that Manning first attempted a written sermon, and then with some uncertainty "On acct. of a tradition that remains among the People about reading Sermons."[11] The great moment came but Manning, fearing that he would alienate his congregation, did not dare to use his prepared notes.[12]

Such divisions in thinking between clergy and congregations extended beyond the field of informal education. In 1827, a perplexed young licentiate wrote from New Brunswick that at the association meeting

> the Brethren . . . very unexpectedly advised me to leave all behind and repair to Either Waterville, or Newton College and spend at least three years in Studying, Moreover these good brethering who have spent many years in the ministry. . . Endeavoured to prove to me by their Experience and did not hesitate to confidently affirm that if I negglected going it would hereafter become a matter of regret to me and would be perpetually regretted through life.

However, when he returned to his pastorate at Lubec, he found his people very hostile to the idea.[13]

It would seem clear that any delay in moving toward a more formal education for the clergy and for the laity in general originated not in the opposition of the majority of the clergy but in the anti-intellectual traditions of the congregations. The objections raised to formal education seem to have fallen into five broad categories, which were, of course, not unrelated, and sprang largely from the Maritime experience.

The first of these objections was the often expressed fear that learning — human knowledge — would be exalted over piety, would in fact replace it, or as one writer expressed it, "substituting human attainments for the assistance of the Holy Spirit. . . ."[14] One writer to the *Christian Messenger* in 1838 expressed the fear that "a race of young pedants, in the character of christian ministers, might be raised up as our future preachers and spiritual guides, after 'the fathers' had fallen asleep and were no more."[15] A lay preacher, writing from New Brunswick, expressed the belief that when young men destined for the ministry go to a seminary they "soon lose all sense of the great work before them; their love is cold, their religion is formality, their exertions feeble in the cause of God."[16] Harris Harding expressed well this fear when, as he lay dying, he was informed of the arrival of an educated clergyman in Yarmouth. He snapped: "I wonder what people mean by sending to England and Scotland for ministers, with their Latin, and Greek, and Hebrew." Then, realizing that he spoke to a man of similar attainments, Harding voiced his real fears. "Oh," he said, "I don't object to the Latin, and Greek, and Hebrew, but let them be placed at the *feet* of Jesus, and not inscribed, as by Pilate, over his head."[17] Even Edward Manning was not untouched by such reservations concerning formal education. In 1828 he wrote to a friend:

> I certainly would recommend to you and every other young Minister to avail themselves of every opportunity to improve their minds in every branch of useful knowledge but to beware of every study,

and every pursuit that would have a tendancy directly or indirectly to lead the mind away from God.[18]

The second often repeated objection was closely allied to the first. The Fathers, it was argued, without the benefit of formal training, had conducted revivals, raised churches and developed the denomination. Conversely, it was claimed, the Established Church was filled with educated men and it had availed them nothing in past years.[19] As one writer observed: "Those old Ministers had no college learning, and the Lord has blessed their preaching as greatly as if they had had ever so much."[20] In general, this objection to education could be called the it-was-good-enough-for-our-fathers view.

It was also felt by many that there was no time for formal training. While a young man wasted his time with three or four years of college work, thousands of people in the Maritimes would die without Christ. Which was more important, it was asked, book learning or soul winning?[21] The fields were white unto harvest; surely the labourers should not tarry over their books. So at least ran the argument.

These three objections were aimed specifically at the idea of education for the clergy. The next two dealt with the broader implication of education for the community at large. The first of these was probably the more telling — and the most difficult of all the objections to answer. Many argued that, simply stated, education had little or no real relevance in the daily lives of most Baptists in the Maritime colonies. The time and money required for collegiate training could be far better spent in acquiring property and experience. One advocate of education attacked this issue in the pages of the *Baptist Missionary Magazine* when he wrote:

I have been filled with astonishment to discover so little zeal in parents, and even Christian parents, to educate their children. Confident am I that their zeal is not in proportion to their circumstances; for parents who are careful to provide farms for their sons, can satisfy their conscience in permitting them to commence the business of life in a state of comparative ignorance, unqualified for the society of any but the low and the vulgar.[22]

The Baptists of the Maritimes would demand that the utilitarianism of education be demonstrated before they would become supporters of institutions of learning.

The last objection raised against education dealt with the ideas and influences disseminated by teachers and professors. Colleges and schools propagated new and therefore probably dangerous and disturbing ideas — religious, social and political. The fact that it was to the United States that some of the Maritime Baptists looked for educational leadership caused much disquiet among their brethren. When word spread that the recently established Horton Academy would be headed by a young minister from the United States, a New Brunswicker wrote with some concern to Edward Manning seeking clarification on certain important points. It being a common impression in his part of the country that all American Baptist ministers were members of the secret Masonic Order, the inquirer wished to know if that "Mistress of Darkness" was to be embraced by and taught in the new academy at Horton. If so, he would have nothing to do with it.[23] Manning shared some of these reservations about American influences. In commenting on the arrival of a new schoolmaster at Cornwallis, Manning observed that he "Is a man of intelligence, but I feel a little cautious about him. He's been in America before."[24] This is an interesting and revealing comment from a man who himself had "been in America before!" There is an undercurrent of anti-Americanism in the Maritimes that allied itself to other anti-educational arguments being advanced in the early decades of the nineteenth century.

Perhaps summing up all the accumulated feelings concerning education is an obituary which appeared in the *Christian Messenger* in 1838. The young man in question had "impaired his constitution by unremitting application to study and literary pursuits."[25]

Although the foregoing objections to education by no means disappeared from the scene, by the second and third decades of the 19th century they were beginning to be successfully challenged by other, conflicting, ideas on the subject. In this revolution in thinking, the Baptist clergy in general played a very conspicuous role, often proving themselves far ahead of their own congregations. A number of forces, acting together, brought about this change in the climate of opinion which led to the founding of Horton Academy, the Fredericton Seminary and Acadia College in such rapid succession.

By the late teens and early twenties of the new century, the Fathers had, with years of searching and frequent conflict, worked out among themselves a basic body of beliefs and church practice. Although all did not yet run smoothly, the roughest days of uncertainty and dissension seemed to lie behind them. Out of the scattered Methodist, Congregational, Anglican and other backgrounds of those involved, they had evolved to a basic understanding of the Baptist position. There was, by the 1820s, such a thing as a Regular Baptist orthodoxy in the Maritime colonies. To protect what had been achieved by such unremitting labour, it would be necessary to pass on to the new generation of ministers the accumulated wisdom of the Fathers.

All of the Regular Baptist ministers had to contend, from time to time, with the arrival in their areas of new preachers who would attempt to woo their congregations from them. Manning described one such intruder as

> the means of moving the People's minds, but he appears to be quite untaught and consequently unskillful, and while I hope he does good he is liable to do a great deal of hurt by taking everything for gold that glistens, and not discriminating between true and false affections, and not teaching the people what they ought to be taught....[26]

Another he described as "a man of some ability, but an unsound man."[27] That the populace in general appeared very willing to listen to such men is all too clear. Manning, in a list of the things which distressed him about his fellow Baptists, included this:

6th. An itching of ears to hear strange preachers, and not being well instructed are liable to be imposed upon by a man of gifts and false zeal. . . .[28]

It was, then, both an uneducated preacher and an ignorant congregation that were to be feared in this new era.

The 1835 Report of the Nova Scotia Baptist Education Committee underscored the need of education to provide continuity in the transition from the aging Fathers to the newer ministers. The Report stated, in part:

> By individual effort, guided by the Holy Spirit, [the Fathers] have wrought out for themselves, much of the knowledge which it is the object of seminaries rather to *facilitate* than to give....they possess a degree of real education, without which, acquired either by similar labours, or supplied by the advantages of previous mental culture, no young minister will be competent to fill their place, as they are successively removed to their rest above. It is a matter of fact, that education as directed in places of learning does *facilitate* the acquisition, in the course of a few years, of that sort of knowledge which our elder brethren possess as the fruit of a long life, and the result of much painful experience; . . . .[29]

The desire to provide stability, to protect the Baptist position from assaults from the evangelical left and to assure that the struggles of the Fathers would not have been in vain all clearly demanded both a better educated clergy and a well informed laity.

If there was growing concern about successful attacks from the evangelical sector, as the Baptists became more firmly established they also concerned themselves more and more with a defence of their position from the criticism of the more conservative elements of the Christian Church. In earlier days, they had sought merely to brush aside the aspersions of Anglicans, Presbyterians and others. By the 1820s, there was a growing desire among some of the Baptist clergy to use their enemies' own weapon — education — against them. Samuel

Elder wrote to Edward Manning in 1826, stating that they desperately needed someone learned in Greek and Latin to answer the charges leveled by the pedobaptists. However, they would have to send someone to Waterville, Maine, to get the necessary aid.[30]

In a similar vein, a correspondent to the *Christian Messenger* in 1837 stated:

> The time is fresh in my recollections, and in many of yours also, when we were but a feeble band. Our defenceless condition invited the hostility of our enemies, and we were obliged in silence to hear our principles misrepresented, and our character, as a Demonination traduced and reviled. I, myself, have often silently groaned under the calumnies which I knew to be industriously circulated by the enemies of the Baptists, because I had not the ability to meet the persons even handed who committed the wrong. Our condition has now happily changed. Men are found in our ranks, fully equal to our defence.[31]

The desire to be more respectable, to be able to defend themselves against attacks from without, thus proved a powerful incentive in the intellectual change overtaking the Baptist community. As one writer succinctly phrased it: "We must not only not despise learning, but must resolve that Satan shall not have the sole use of it."[32]

Not only were the Baptists increasingly aware of the need of training for the rising generation of clergy, but they were becoming acutely aware of the danger that the United States posed in this regard. The growing fear that the bright young men of the Maritimes would be lured off to New England for an education and never return was another reason for the establishment of suitable institutions in their own region. E. A. Crawley used just such an argument in 1838 to justify the founding of Queen's College. He wrote, in part:

> Our young men are at present leaving us, to seek, in other countries, a more advanced education. Their return is problematical, and, the threatened loss to the

97

community in the abstraction of cultivated talent and industry, not trivial.[33]

The Address of the Committee of the Nova Scotia Baptist Education Society for the same year spoke of the current "banishment of those cultivated minds which have been our brightest hope."[34] When promising young men such as John Pryor, Edmund Crawley and Isaac Chipman went to the United States to study, there was always the fear that they would never return. The situation would only worsen in the future if steps were not taken to rectify the problem.

It is clear that the dramatic events in Halifax, 1825-28, greatly influenced the educational attitudes of Maritime Baptists. The disruption in St. Paul's Anglican Church and the eventual founding of the Granville Street Baptist Church brought to the Baptist denomination men of elevated social standing and considerable education. Many of the Baptist leaders saw these events as very significant in the growth of the denomination.[35] It was realized that if the Baptists were to attract and hold people of such standing, a more educated clergy would be essential. This was brought home forcefully and painfully to the ministers of the denomination when the "new" Baptists of Halifax sent to the United States for a clergyman to constitute their church and become their pastor.[36] The Nova Scotia Education Society in 1832 begged

> the youthful candidates for ministerial service to believe, it is no less certain, that there are stations, and will be many more, where it is of vast importance to place labourers uniting *education* and *piety*.[37]

If the Baptist denomination of the Maritimes hoped ever to extend its influence beyond the lower classes, steps would have to be taken to provide for an educated clergy.

The events in Halifax influenced what might be described as the rising expectations of Maritime Baptists. As long as they had been content with their essentially lower class positions, there would appear to be little reason for an extensive education. By the 1820s and 1830s, many Baptists were no longer prepared to accept the social gradations that
98

had previously prevailed in these colonies. Education, it was felt, could be the key to a future of Baptist advancement. These sentiments were conveyed to the public in 1835 in the Report of the Nova Scotia Baptist Education Society. It was argued:

> If the youth of this Province are to fill with credit the various municipal or professional offices which the country requires — if they are to be skillful physicians, successful lawyers, or intelligent merchants; if, as jury men, they are to decide with wisdom in difficult causes, where the property or the life of a fellow being hangs on their judgment — if, as magistrates, they are to exercise their high office with dignity and discretion — or as the representatives of the people, they are to represent, not merely the will or the wealth, but the wisdom of their fellow subjects, and really to legislate for the public *good* — in all these cases, it will be admitted, that they need in greater or lesser degree a due portion of judicious, well directed education.[38]

There is more than a hint of class conflict in such statements.

Anti-establishment feelings were expressed even more clearly in a letter to the Nova Scotia Baptist Association from "A True Friend of the Horton Academy." In response to the attacks of an Anglican clergyman on Horton Academy, "A True Friend" wrote pointedly:

> He [the Anglican clergyman] knows the influence which education enables those who possess it to exert, and he consequently well knows the advantages which the Baptists are to derive from the Institutions at Horton. He sees in the distance, and not very dimly either, a host of young men coming forth from that place of learning, and spreading themselves over the country, who are to advocate those principles of civil and religious liberty which he affects to despise, and to grapple successfully with those who have hitherto engrossed the wealth and influence of the country, and who have employed these, so far as

education is concerned, in closing up the avenues to knowledge against Dissenters. . . .[39]

Education and advancement were becoming linked in the minds of many Baptists. This would cause them to see as even more sinister the attempts by the elite to keep education out of the hands of the masses.

Coupled with this feeling that education provided the avenue for personal and denominational advancement was another argument for the development of institutions of higher learning. Maritimers were increasingly aware of the changes taking place in the world around them and they expressed the growing conviction that they must not be left behind. As an 1838 editorial in the *Christian Messenger* argued, in our "advanced state of society" it was necessary to provide much better educational facilities "if we have any desire of keeping pace with the age in which we live. . . ."[40] The colonial period was behind them, it was argued; the time when "native energy rather than cultural talent" would suffice was past. In 1838, it was observed that

> if the improvements, enterprize, and wealth, which characterize this age of the civilized world, are to be transplanted in any just proportion to our shores, it will be effected fully as much by raising the scale of intellectual cultivation, as by exercising the labours of industry, or developing the natural resources of the country.[41]

The advancement, indeed the transformation, of the world was at stake. If light and learning were to spread throughout the world, if missionaries were to be sent to heathen lands, if oppression and darkness were to be expelled, then education must be encouraged.

Throughout much of this runs an obvious thread of class consciousness, and of impending change. The 1832 report of the Nova Scotia Baptist Education Society expressed the current understanding of world trends and the important role of education:

100

Without venturing near the borders of political discussion, which certainly ought never to stain the pages of such a report as the present, it is however obvious, *as a fact*, that a great change is gradually, and yet, perhaps, not slowly, taking place in the political horizon of t'ie civilized world: that Governments are rapidly leaning to the popular form; and the people every where acquiring a great increase of power.

But who could wish such power to be thrown into the hands of an ignorant and degraded people? Such must inevitably be exposed to the arts of designing men, who would soon ride over their necks as arbitrary despots — witness the tyrant of Corsica — witness the hundred tyrants, perpetually crushed and reproduced in Southern America.

On this subject there are two parties in the world, one contending for only a partial enlightening of the people, and for retaining power in the hands of the few, through the influence of ancient usages — the other, struggling to diffuse knowledge, to effect reformation, and professing to examine ancient usages by the test of principle and right.[42]

There must be no doubt, it was argued, as to the position occupied by Maritime Baptists in this emerging confrontation.

The desire to provide continuity, to defend the denomination from attack, to avoid the lures of the United States, and to provide the opportunity for individual and world wide advancement combined with the catalytic forces at work in Halifax to transform the Baptist community from a powerful anti-intellectual force to one of the foremost advocates of universal education to be found in the Maritime colonies. The Baptists were by no means united in this cause; the older views died only slowly or not at all. However, the new forces proved more powerful. By 1840 education was viewed in far different terms than it had been fifty or even twenty years before, and it could now be used as an important tool in the further advancement of the denomination. An 1838 editorial best summarized the new, all-encompassing views of

101

education:

> We ought therefore never to forget the solemn duty we owe to ourselves, to our children, to the world at large, to promote to the utmost of our ability the cause of education, which, in its widest and best sense, is the cause of humanity, and the cause of God.[43]

The New Brunswick Baptist Seminary 1833 - 1895

ALLISON A. TRITES

The 1820's and 30's were bustling days in colonial New Brunswick. The shipbuilders of Saint John were entering a period of unbelievable prosperity. The lumber tycoons of the province were busy exploiting the forests and exporting timber to Britain on preferential terms. The merchants of Saint John were expanding their trade and importing goods from the West Indies as well as from Britain and the United States. The farmers were settling the beautiful river valleys of the province and opening up the rugged interior. The politicians were engaged in a bitter struggle over the disposition of the Crown lands. And the evangelists of the Christian faith were on the move, planting churches in the vast hinterland of the colony.[1]

I. THE NEED OF A SEMINARY

At the beginning of the nineteenth century, New Brunswick Baptists were a tiny force in this young province. They had established small churches in scattered communities in the central and southern portions of the province, but their efforts were hamstrung by the lack of trained leadership. The churches which had sprung to life through the efforts of Henry Alline and the Baptist Fathers[2] were gradually losing the first flush of evangelistic enthusiasm, and were in danger of lapsing into a period of spiritual carelessness. Thus in the Association's Corresponding Letter for 1830 the Moderator, the Rev. F.W. Miles, bemoaned the fact

> . . .that our Churches are living far below their exalted privileges — that revivals and reformations are less frequent and encouraging than formerly — and that clouds and darkness surround the throne of the Eternal.[3]

Among the Baptist pastors and lay leaders there was a real desire that the churches might be awakened to a deeper and more abiding concern for the extensive spread of the gospel.[4] With this desire "to promote truth in the earth, and the spread of the gospel which shall bless every land"[5], there arose the conviction that it was necessary to train people for Christian leadership if these evangelistic and missionary aims were to be realized.[6] This did not mean the development of an exclusively theological school for the professional training of ministers, for the times were not ripe for such an institution.[7] Rather, the school was

> . . .established for the purpose of disseminating the blessings of useful information generally among the youth of the province — a special object being to induce young men who might feel it to be their duty to devote themselves to the Christian ministry, to attend at the Institution and obtain a good English education, at least, and to proceed farther should circumstances admit, and eventually to establish a regular theological department and require such students to go a given time.[8]

II. THE ESTABLISHMENT OF THE SEMINARY

The actual creation of the New Brunswick Baptist Seminary took place in 1833. Frederick W. Miles and W.B.

Kinnear had embraced the Baptist position, and were eager to share the benefits of higher education with their Baptist friends and their children. They promoted the idea of establishing a Baptist seminary of learning in New Brunswick, and found a ready response in men such as C.D. Everett in Saint John, George Miles in Maugerville, and Jarvis Ring, William Estey, Aaron Hartt, John T. Smith and Z.G. Gabel in Fredericton.[9] When the New Brunswick Baptist Association met for its annual meeting in St. George in.July 1833, there was a great deal of discussion about the need for such a school. "Encouraged by the success of the Horton Academy and realizing that a seminary was essential to the success of the denomination both at home and in foreign lands, the Association accepted the proposal [of Miles and Kinnear]...."[10] Thirty-four laymen, together with all the ordained Baptist ministers of the province were named to a general committee to promote the seminary plan. A special committee was established to prepare a prospectus,[11] and a meeting was arranged for the fall.

Thus in 1833 the Baptists of New Brunswick with a numerical strength of only 1721[12] managed to establish an institution of higher education which was to survive in a variety of forms and locations for over sixty years. In September 1833 a public meeting was held in Saint John, at which time the formal organization of the New Brunswick Baptist Education Society took place, and the Rev. Joseph Crandall of Salisbury was elected President.[13] According to its original constitution (1833), the purpose of the Society was "the Establishment and Maintenance of a Seminary of Learning at Maugerville, under the management of the Committee and supervision of the Board of Directors." The goal was "to provide pious and efficient teachers, under whose care and that of the Committee it shall be an all-important object to inculcate sound religious and moral principles, and to induce habits of industry, good order and economy." The stated intention was to "afford the means of instruction in the usual branches of English literature, and of scientific, classical and other studies, which usually comprise the course of education at an academy, theological seminary and college."[14]

When the original site in Maugerville proved to be unsuitable for building, it was decided to construct the premises of the new seminary in Fredericton[15] on the corner of York and George Streets, on a plot of land adjacent to what is now Brunswick St. United Baptist Church.[16] The actual work on the building began in 1834,[17] and was finished in 1835 at a cost of $9,504, including lands and fences.[18] The construction was undertaken by Messrs. Burpee and Taylor of Sheffield, who later complained that the altered location had cost them dearly and appealed unsuccessfully for redress.[19]

III. THE EARLY YEARS OF THE SEMINARY

The Seminary opened its doors for instruction on January 4th, 1836, with the Rev. F.W. Miles as Principal and his wife as Preceptress in charge of the Female Department.[20] Young men and women were admitted on equal terms, and "in this respect the Baptist Seminary at Fredericton pioneered for all Canada."[21]   Admission was open to students of all denominations, and no religious tests were required.[22] This did not mean, however, that the institution was unconcerned about maintaining high standards. The Annual Report of the Education Society for 1836 stated that "the strictest attention to moral and Christian principles has been enforced", but this was done "without regard to the peculiarities of sect or party".[23]

The financial problems which were to plague the school throughout its history were present from its earliest days.[24] To alleviate the pressure, it was considered advisable to apply for a grant from the New Brunswick Legislature. For a number of years this grant was passed by the Legislative Assembly, only to be rejected by the Legislative Council.[25] Apparently the upper house thought such a grant would be injurious to the growth and development of King's College, the precursor of the modern University of New Brunswick. Unfortunately, King's College at that time favored Anglicans[26], so the discriminatory basis on which higher education was conducted in the province was one of the factors which contributed to the
106

formation of both the Baptist Seminary in Fredericton and the Wesleyan Academy in Sackville.[27]

The early years of the Seminary were "extremely arduous". Since funds were limited, the first year Mr. and Mrs. Miles had to cope on their own with seventy students.[28] Like many of their successors, they literally wore themselves out in the service of the school. Charlotte Miles, who had worked so loyally and effectively in the opening days, had to resign due to ill health. She died in December, 1837.[29] However, by 1837 the Committee of Management could report that Mr. J.W. Hartt and Miss P.B. Brown had been employed as Assistant Teachers in the Male and Female Departments respectively. Miss Brown became Principal of the Female Department in the place of Mrs. Miles.

Due to the loss of his wife and a deterioration in his own health, F.W. Miles resigned as Principal in 1838.[30] His place was taken by the Rev. Charles Tupper, one of the most famous men in the history of Atlantic Baptists.[31] This self-taught scholar, pastor, editor and teacher held the principalship for just fifteen months, relinquishing the position to the former Principal on the latter's return from England in October 1839.[32] Unfortunately Miles was able to resume the leadership of the Seminary for only six months, when his health failed him once again. He died prematurely on February 2, 1842, in his thirty-seventh year, widely respected and deeply loved both as the pastor of the Fredericton Baptist Church and as the driving force and first Principal of the Seminary.[33]

When Principal Miles was compelled by ill health to retire from his labours early in 1840, Mr. Hartt the Assistant Teacher finished out the year with the male students. The Female School was then under the capable leadership of Miss Bennett, of England, who was succeeded by Mrs. W.H. Needham and Mrs. Akerley, of Fredericton. The Committee of Management appointed a Baptist layman to succeed Miles as the new Principal.[34] Charles Randall was a native of Nova Scotia, and subsequently was to enjoy a useful teaching career in his native province. His tenure was short, for at the close of the spring term in 1842 he resigned, apparently on the grounds of ill health.[35] Later he returned to Nova Scotia to become the

Principal of Horton Academy. However, when Randall instituted a lawsuit to obtain back wages, he incurred the displeasure of the officers of the New Brunswick Baptist Education Society, who felt that he had acted in a selfish manner unbecoming of a Christian and unworthy of a fellow Baptist![36]

Once again Charles Tupper stepped into the breach, serving for a term as interim Principal as well as pastor of the Fredericton Baptist Church. He was succeeded briefly by the Rev. William Hall, who also taught for one term at the low remuneration of twenty-five pounds, twelve pounds 5 shillings of which he gave as a donation to the Society![37] Although it would have been comparatively easy to have found an American, the Committee of Management thought it important that "the person filling that office should be one entertaining the political feeling and predilections of the Country", and therefore decided to look for a new Principal in Great Britain.[38]

In response to inquiries made in England through the Baptist Colonial Missionary Society, the name of the Rev. Charles Spurden was recommended to the officers of the Fredericton academy.[39] Spurden, a native of London and a recent graduate of Bristol (Baptist) College, had been recently ordained in Hereford, and had devoted himself for a year and a half to the pastoral ministry there when the call came to come to New Brunswick to head the fledgling institution. He had already impressed some leading British Baptists with his academic and spiritual qualities, and arrived in New Brunswick in December of 1842 with the highest of recommendations.[40] His North American colleagues were not to be disappointed, for in Charles Spurden they found the man who was to give solid, steady and unwearied devotion to the New Brunswick Baptist Seminary for the rest of his life.[41]

The next few years were ones of quiet steady progress.[42] In 1845 Thomas B. Smith was appointed as Assistant Teacher, a post which he ably filled for eight years. He in turn was succeeded by A.H. Munro, a fine teacher who rendered two years of valuable service to the school.[43] The proposal made at the Eastern Association in Hillsborough in 1853 was not carried into effect, so the school had to limp along with its debt of five hundred and seventy-five pounds and interest charges of approximately thirty pounds per year. The Female Department, which had been closed after the winter term in 1843, was reopened in 1857, and several years later Miss C. Magee of Calais, Maine, was hired as Preceptress. By 1865 there were three teachers — Dr. Spurden the Principal, John E. Hopper, the "Classical and Mathematical Professor", and J. Jones, "English Master". The next year Messers Goodspeed, Wilbur and Bill were added to the teaching staff. The academic year was divided into four terms of eleven weeks each, and fees were set at $128, $132 and $136, depending on the age of the pupil.

In March 1857, Principal Spurden was given a year's leave of absence, during which he travelled to England to visit friends and seek the renewal of his wife's health. In his absence, the Rev. Isaiah Wallace, an Acadia graduate and an effective evangelist, served as interim Principal until Spurden returned in July, 1858.[44] George E. Day held the post of Assistant Teacher for two years, resigning in 1859; he was later to obtain his M.D. degree and serve as a prominent Maritime Baptist minister.[45]

IV. THE CLOSING YEARS OF THE FREDERICTON SEMINARY

In 1866 Dr. Spurden became "Professor of Theology and Hebrew" and J.E. Hopper now took up the duties of "Principal and Classical and Mathematical Tutor".[46] The following year Spurden had to resign on account of ill health after twenty-four years of devoted service. Tragically, there were no students in the Theological Department to which he had agreed to devote his full attention! In paying tribute to Dr. Spurden the Committee of Management expressed their "high estimation of his qualities as a Teacher, and of his upright, amiable and excellent character during the whole of that time, while zealously and devotedly discharging the duties of Principal of the Seminary."[47]

John Hopper, a graduate of Acadia College (1862), took up the reins of office. After three years' service as

Principal (1866-69), Hopper left to become the first pastor of the Baptist Church in St. Stephen, N.B.[48] Other teachers on the staff at the time were George E. Tufts and Luther E. Wortman, who later joined the faculty of Acadia as Professor of French and German.[49] The Female Department in 1869 was under the care of Miss Rosie A. Bentley, who later married Richard H. Phillips, the clerk of the Fredericton Baptist Church (1869-71).

In 1869 the Rev. Calvin Goodspeed, a native of Nashwaak, N.B., was named to succeed Hopper,[50] and to him fell the unenviable task of presiding over the institution as it faced its most threatening crisis.

The *coup de grace* was delivered to the already ailing institution when the Legislature of New Brunswick passed the Common School Act in 1871. When the Eastern New Brunswick Baptist Association met in July 1872, the question was raised as to whether the Seminary should continue as a feeder to Acadia College, or whether it should be discontinued in the light of changed circumstances.[51]

The Directors of the Baptist Education Society met in July 1872 and unanimously resolved "that the Baptist Seminary at Frederiction be handed over to the Committee of Management for one year, for the purpose of educating young men for the ministry."[52] Dr. Spurden was again made Principal and Professor of Theology.[53]

The experiment in theological education was unsuccessful, however,[54] and in June 1873, when the Western New Brunswick Association met at Keswick, York Co., it was resolved that

> ...the property in Fredericton, known as the Baptist Seminary, be sold for the highest possible price, and money securely invested, to be appropriated for educational purposes as the Denomination in this Province shall direct.[55]

The next year when the Eastern Association met at Elgin, Albert Co., in July 1874, the Committee of Management of the Seminary reported that

...the building and lands according to the resolution of the Directors were sold to the trustees of schools, Fredericton for the sum of $5,000, payable in school debentures, bearing interest at six per cent, to commence January 1st, 1874.[56]

The furniture was also sold and the library was placed in the Baptist parsonage in Fredericton for safe keeping.

The closure and sale of the Fredericton Seminary marked the end of the first phase of the school's life. Dr. Herbert Creed summarized the contribution of the Fredericton Seminary in this way:

> Its career lasted about thirty-seven years. It did a good work in its day. There some hundreds of young persons of both sexes enjoyed good educational advantages. Many young men passed from the Seminary to College, the most of them to the University at Fredericton. Some entered the ministry, and have since rendered valuable service as preachers and pastors.[57] Within the walls of the old Seminary many respected Christian teachers labored faithfully and self-sacrificingly. From Dr. Bill's History [and from the Annual Reports of the New Brunswick Baptist Education Society to the Western New Brunswick Baptist Association] we learn that the average attendance, after twenty years of existence, was from 46 to 50. The maintenance of the Seminary was a continued financial struggle. Debt burdened the institution, especially in its later years.[58]

While some thought that the school had served its purpose and should die an honorable death,[59] others were to take up the cause of higher education and to give the New Brunswick Baptist Seminary a new lease on life in a new location.

V. THE RESUMPTION OF THE SEMINARY IN SAINT JOHN

Agitation for the reopening of the school developed in

the late seventies after the return of the Rev. J.E. Hopper from his residence in Burlington, Iowa. When the Western New Brunswick Baptist Association met in Rockland, Carleton Co., in June 1879, it was noted in the Report of the Committee of Education that

> ...while we rejoice in the prosperity of the Horton Academy we cannot close our report without expressing the hope that the day is not far distant when we shall have, in our own Province, an Academy affiliated with Acadia College, at which our young men may conveniently prepare themselves for that Institution, and be useful, meanwhile, in supplying some of our numerous destitute fields with the preaching of the Gospel.[60]

A similar concern was voiced when the Eastern New Brunswick Baptist Association met in Harvey, Albert Co., in July 1881. On that occasion the Committee on Education commented:

> We are pleased to learn that the desire for the re-opening of the Baptist Seminary in this Province is becoming stronger, and trust that in the near future the funds held by the New Brunswick Baptist Education Society will be used with others donated for the purpose to provide an Academic Institution in this Province affiliated with Acadia College.[61]

The next year these concerns blossomed into action in St. George, the very place where the old Fredericton Seminary had been conceived forty-nine years previously. On June 15, 1882, the Southern Association met there for its annual meeting and resolved:

> That this Association expresses its firm belief that the time for the New Brunswick Baptist Education Society to resume its work of providing a Seminary for our sons and daughters has fully arrived, and we urge it to take such action to effect this end, as it shall deem wisest and best.[62]

112

The Eastern Association, meeting at Havelock in July of that year, made a similar report and resolution, which were enthusiastically adopted by unanimous vote.[63]

Thus with the support of the Associations there was a real effort made to reopen the institution. A committee had been appointed on September 15, 1881, to explore the possibility and on August 18, 1882, presented its favorable report to the Board of Management.

The revived Seminary opened in temporary quarters in Saint John on October 10, 1882, with a new Principal, W.M. McVicar, who was just concluding his service as Principal of the Model School in Truro.[64] Berryman's Building on the corner of Princess and Germain Streets provided the school with attractive and well appointed premises. Four classrooms were used, and a large assembly hall was available for special occasions.[65] Out-of-town students were housed in boarding establishments approved by the school. Thus in October 1882 the Baptist Seminary "awoke to new life and vigor, and started forth upon a new career."[66]

At the outset no regular course was prescribed. Later two divisions were organized and in September 1883 a three year diploma course was instituted. According to a contemporary newspaper account,

>...the course comprises two divisions — a Classical and a Literary. The former is intended for students who purpose entering College. The Literary Course is designed to afford thorough and complete training to young ladies and gentlemen who are not intending to enter College, but who are seeking a good degree of literary culture.[67]

During its first year in Saint John, the Seminary taught 84 students, 31 young men and 53 young women. The next year there were 80 students registered, and arrangements were made to rent a large building for use as a boarding residence.

In October 1883 New Brunswick Baptists appointed a committee to meet with the Free Christian Baptists to propose a union of the two denominations in educational work. The committee was warmly received by the Free Baptists [68] and a basis of union was drawn up which declared that "each body would raise one-half a sum sufficient to build and furnish an institution, that each body elect half the board of directors; that until a new building should be erected, the joint directorate control the school."[69] This basis of union was adopted by the Baptist Education Society. So when the Seminary opened in the autumn of 1884, it was under the joint control of the Regular Baptists of New Brunswick and the Free Christian Baptists. The New Brunswick Baptist Education Society was renamed "The Union Baptist Education Society."

For a number of years the Seminary continued to thrive with enrollments of 81 in 1885 and 100 in 1886,[70] while its Directors were selecting and preparing a permanent school. The Jewett property, a magnificent estate on Carleton Heights in the Parish of Lancaster, was purchased for the sum of $35,000, but it was considered to be unsuitable for the Seminary's purposes and was resold.[71] After due consideration, "it was thought best to remove the school to some country place, away from the attractions and temptations of the City."[72]

VI. THE FINAL YEARS OF THE SEMINARY — ST. MARTINS

Several places were suggested as possible locations for the Seminary, including Moncton, Sussex and St. Martins. Finally in August 1886 the decision was made to locate in St. Martins[73] when Captain George Masters offered a generous gift of $10,000 on the condition that the institution be located in that village. In addition, $6,000 was contributed by other residents of the community.

The plans for an impressive structure were prepared by Mr. H.H. Mott, a gifted Maritime architect.[74] The contract for the construction of the building in red brick, set off with trimmings of freestone, was awarded to Messrs. Causey and Maxwell for $25,575.[75] Unfortunately, the building was to prove far too expensive for the Baptists of New Brunswick to

114

maintain in solvent condition, even with the help of the Free Christian Baptists.

The cornerstone was laid by Captain George Masters in July 1886, but the building was not ready for occupancy until September 1888. The vast structure was really three buildings under one roof. With its gargantuan dimensions (217 ft. long, 130 ft. deep, with three stories and a basement) it was in its day "without question the largest and best equipped school building in the Maritime Provinces."[76] However, the full cost of the building and its furnishings, taking into account the vast sums paid out in servicing the debt, amounted to $65,000.[77]

From the start, the St. Martins operation was financially unstable. The first Principal in the new building, the Rev. B.F. Simpson,[78] remained only one year (1888-89), leaving the already troubled institution with an enlarged debt. During the summer of 1889 the position was offered to the Rev. J.E. Hopper, who had served the institution some twenty years earlier in Fredericton. Now he was summoned to lead the school in a time of financial crisis, bringing with him all his business, professional and administrative skill.[79] Dr. Hopper accepted the Principal's position, and under his astute leadership the Seminary revived. Money from interested friends came in, and some of the debt was retired.[80]

In December 1891 the school held a public meeting celebrating the completion of the $15,000 subscription list. Dr. Hopper was honoured at a reception at the Seminary on his fiftieth birthday. On that occasion he stated publicly:

> I thank God for three things in connection with our Seminary: first for the Union in which it rests, then for the dignity that (through the system of co-education) it puts upon woman, and finally for the way in which it honors the Bible by the place assigned it in the course....Today our Seminary has scarcely an opponent in the Province of New Brunswick. Strife has ceased and all are for us.[81]

Dr. Hopper worked indefatigably for the Seminary, but finally had to retire, worn out after three years of capable

115

leadership (1889-92). As he reluctantly laid down his office, Dr. Hopper confessed: "The financial strain in securing the $15,000 and the conduct of the school since, has been such as to exhaust my strength and nervous power."[82] His place was taken by Austin Kennedy de Blois, Ph.D., the son of a prominent Maritime Baptist minister, Dr. Stephen de Blois.[83] The financial burdens of the school were still serious, but were of "manageable proportions".[84]

Like his predecessor, Dr. de Blois spared no pains to put the Seminary on a sound financial foundation, but his efforts met with only limited success. In reviewing his own work on behalf of the school at the end of the 1892-93 academic year, Dr. de Blois said that "he had written 1,100 letters, travelled 6,000 miles by railway and 1,200 by private conveyance, and addressed some 40 public gatherings in the interests of the school."[85] At the same time he attempted to place the Seminary on a firm academic foundation, viewing the school as essentially a preparatory institution.[86]

The Union Baptist Seminary Calendar of 1893-94 proudly announced that its faculty consisted of fifteen full time teachers and seven part-time lecturers. Its student body, drawn from all three Maritime Provinces and the United States, numbered 104 and spanned five denominations. Nine of the 104 students were registered as theological students.

As in Saint John, there were several courses of study. Each course took three years, and diplomas were awarded on the successful completion of the curriculum. The aspiring college student was directed to the Matriculation Course, which entitled those who completed it to admission to the freshman class of Acadia University and similar institutions without examination. The Classical Course was designed for students who did not wish to pursue "so extended a course as the College provides," but "who nevertheless desire a broad and practical training to fit them for the duties of life." It included "the study of Latin or French in the Freshman year, and any two languages in the Junior and Senior years, besides English, Science, and advanced Mathematics."[87] Another option was the English-Scientific Course.[88]

There were also Departments of Music and Elocution

116

(where instruction was given in piano, organ, violin and voice), not to speak of the practical Departments of Art, Needlework and Business. A real attempt to prepare some students for a vocation is indicated by the inclusion of such subjects as typing, shorthand, arithmetic, bookkeeping, telegraphy and penmanship in the curriculum.

The academic year covered thirty-six weeks, and the total cost of tuition, board, laundry and miscellaneous items was $151.00. Pupils attending the Preparatory Department from the community paid only 40¢ a week for tuition and 50¢ a term for fuel.[89]

Each student in residence was expected to provide his own lamp, towels, napkin ring, and bedcovering. The institution furnished each room with "an iron bedstead, a wire-woven spring, bed mattress, bureau commode, and toilet set. Students were usually billeted two to a room."[90]

The Seminary claimed it offered an excellent social life:

> Every Monday evening the teachers and students have a promenade and reception for half an hour in the main corridors. An hour on Tuesday evening is set aside for Prayer Meeting. On Wednesday evening there are games in the Assembly Hall for half an hour, under the direction of a committee of teachers and students. These games are both harmless and interesting and provide a healthful and innocent amusement. On Thursday evening the students have a musical evening for half an hour in the Vocal Music Room where they practise college songs and other melodies. On Friday evening study hours are remitted, and the young men are allowed to visit the Village.[91]

There were a number of extra-curricular organizations in which the students participated. A Seminary Christian Association was officially responsible for the spiritual life of the school. It was aided by the Seminary Missionary Society, which fostered interest in missions and arranged for missionary speakers to visit the campus. The Eclectic Society met regularly on Saturday evenings and offered a wide variety

117

of literary and musical programmes. There was also a Choral Society, a Baseball and Football Club and a Tennis Association.[92] But probably the most distinctive feature of the Seminary was its moral and religious tone:

> The teachers lived among the students and in that way helped to shape and mold their spiritual lives. Every means was taken to promote and foster religious life. Through courses in Bible Study, Prayer Meetings, and frequent missionary gatherings, the students were nurtured in their religious lives. Regular church services and Sunday School were conducted in the chapel every Sunday.[93]

The Calendar of the Seminary plainly declared the Christian stance of the institution:

> The Seminary is not a sectarian but Christian School. No narrow or sectarian elements are present within its walls. Harmony and happiness are characteristic of its life, and no bigoted or false spirit has any place or standing. The name of Jesus Christ is known and honored, and simple trust in a divine Saviour is considered the ground work of true religion, and essential of living faith.[94]

Discipline was a real feature of the school, but judged by the standards of the time, it was not oppressive.[95] It was made very clear to each class that "Our School is not a reformatory and boys or girls with vicious habits are not allowed to contaminate other students by remaining in the School and associating with them."[96] The students of both sexes were permitted to meet in the classrooms and dining halls, but were allowed outside the grounds at the same time only in exceptional circumstances and by special permission.[97]

While the Seminary operated, it undoubtedly provided excellent opportunities for education in a Christian environment.[98] But despite the noble efforts of Principal Willard McIntyre (who assumed the reins of office upon Dr. de Blois' resignation in 1894), the burden of debt finally forced the

118

institution to close its doors.[99]

The records are fragmentary,[100] but there seems to be some evidence of dissension between the two denominations,[101] and the property was sold in 1894 to Mr. G.W. Titus for $2,501 above the mortgage[102] to meet pressing financial obligations of the institution.[103] The Seminary continued to operate in 1894-95, moving into rented premises after Christmas in the hope that some measures might be taken to revive the dying institution. An effort was made to repurchase the Seminary property, but it was unsuccessful, and the School ceased its operations in the spring of 1895.[104]

It is not clear whether the Seminary building changed hands in the next year or two or not. However, according to a tourist brochure published in 1898 and preserved in the Quaco Museum at St. Martins, the Tourist Hotel Company Ltd. with an authorized capital of $45,000 planned to open the Seminary building that autumn.[105] "The building was to accommodate two hundred overnight guests. The hotel was also to hold concerts in an auditorium seating three hundred people. There appears to be no record that the hotel ever opened."[106]

Eventually, the property was purchased by the St. Martins School Board after a fire had destroyed the local school, and for a number of years housed the St. Martins High School. In 1926 two-thirds of the building was taken down, leaving only the left wing standing. This wing has been used in recent years to house the Elementary School in St. Martins until it was demolished by government order in the spring of 1973 after months of heated controversy.[107]

The New Brunswick Baptist Education Society functioned for over sixty years, and made an outstanding contribution to the educational and spiritual life of the Province. The union of the New Brunswick Baptists and the Free Christian Baptists in educational work undoubtedly demonstrated that the two denominations could work together, and from this beginning there developed the Union of 1905-06, resulting in the formation of the Maritime United Baptist Covention.[108] It must be acknowledged that:

119

The Seminary was run successfully and attended by large numbers of students for a few years, but owing to lack of funds, being burdened by a heavy debt, and poor railway communication, it was finally closed in 1895.[109]

The institution had been sustained by much exertion and many prayers. It conferred substantial benefits on the communities in which it was located, and indirectly contributed to the elevation of the standard of education throughout the Province. It sent out into the educational, business and professional worlds a large number of well trained young people instilled with high principles, disciplined and eager to make their contribution to the life of their respective communities. Crippled by financial problems throughout its history, the Seminary was never able to realize its full potential, despite the heroic sacrifice of its teachers and Committee of Management.

It did produce some notable ministers who made their mark on the churches, and several leading educators, among them Calvin Goodspeed, W.M. McVicar, George Foster, Luther Wortman and Shirley Jackson Case.[110] It was guided by some men of outstanding ability, including Charles Spurden, John Hopper and Austin Kennedy de Blois. It was therefore not without a feeling of regret that many New Brunswick Baptists saw the Seminary slip into oblivion after more than half a century of honorable work.[111] As G.R. White remarked in a stirring address on Maritime Baptist educational institutions:

> Under God we owe about all we are as a denomination to these institutions. The fathers went as far as they could without them fifty years ago. The rising generation should not forget the God-given rights that were denied our fathers before they had a college of their own. How well it fits us to glory in our institutions; they have given us freedom to worship God under our own vine and fig tree. Thank God for the faith and courage of the noble men and women that established these institutions. Shall we be recreant to the trust?[112]

About three years before the Seminary went out of existence, C.W. Williams, then Pastor of the St. Martins Baptist Church, had sounded a timely warning:

> If, disregarding God's leadings, we stop before we have altogether passed the difficulty in our way, all is lost; we shall surely be engulfed. To be three-quarters or nine-tenths of the way across the Red Sea is of no avail when the waters come back. Friends of St. Martins, let us for a while yet move *swiftly forward*....None say now that our undertaking [to rescue the Seminary from financial collapse] is impracticable; but there must be much prayer and effort, much liberal giving still. And so, although "the Lord hath done great things for us whereof we are glad" we still cry, "Men of Israel, help."[113]

Sadly, the warning was never fully heeded and the school was engulfed. While determined efforts were made to liquidate the remaining debt, as late as 1898 it had to be admitted that "full settlement" of the outstanding claims had not been achieved.[114]

To many Baptists there was a feeling of shame at the financial collapse of the Union Baptist Seminary. They were concerned at the bad image this failure gave them as a denomination, and wished to remove "the stigma that rests upon us as New Brunswick Baptists." Nevertheless, they looked optimistically beyond the clouds on the present horizon to the prospects of a more hopeful day:

> Let us look forward to the time when we shall again have an academy in this province training our sons and daughters who now seek instruction at other doors. The horizon may look dark just at the present, not even the day-star appearing, but the watchman on the height as you ask, "What of the night?" answers, "The morning cometh."[115]

After fifty-four years their long-cherished dream of "an academy in this province" was realized in the creation of the

121

United Baptist Bible Training School on the outskirts of
Moncton, the forerunner of the present Atlantic Baptist
College.

SEMINARY DATA

The New Brunswick Baptist Education Society formed, 1833
Seminary at Fredericton opened, 1836
Seminary at Fredericton closed, 1873
Baptist Education Society re-organized, 1882
Union Baptist Education Society incorporated, 1884
Seminary at St. Martins opened, 1888
Seminary closed, 1895

PRINCIPALS OF THE NEW BRUNSWICK BAPTIST SEMINARY

I. THE SEMINARY AT FREDERICTON

Rev. Frederick Wiles, M.A.	1835-1840
*Rev. Charles Tupper, D.D.	1838-1839
Mr. Charles D. Randall, M.A.	1840-1842
*Rev. Charles Tupper, D.D. (One Term)	1842
*Rev. Willam Hall (One Term)	1842
Rev. Charles Spurden, D.D.	1842-1866
*Rev. Isaiah Wallace, D.D.	1857-1858
Rev. John E. Hopper, D.D.	1866-1869
Rev. Calvin Goodspeed, D.D.	1869-1871
Rev. Charles Spurden, D.D.	1872-1873

II. THE SEMINARY AT SAINT JOHN

Mr. William M. McVicar, M.A.	1882-1884
Mr. Luther E. Wortman, M.A.	1885-1888

III. THE SEMINARY AT ST. MARTINS

Rev. Benjamin F. Simpson, B.D.	1888-1889
Rev. John E. Hopper, D.D.	1889-1892
Rev. Austen K. deBlois, Ph.D.	1892-1894
Rev. Willard E. McIntyre, D.D.	1894-1895

*Acted as Interim Principal

Alice Shaw
and her Grand Pre Seminary
A Story of Female Education

JAMES DOYLE DAVISON

Lewis Carroll's "Alice in Wonderland" asked the Cheshire-Cat which way she should go from here. "That depends a good deal on where you want to go," said the Cat. "I don't much care where..." said Alice. "Then it doesn't matter which way you go," said the Cat. ". . . so long as I go *somewhere*," Alice added as an explanation. "Oh, you're sure to do that," said the Cat, "if you only walk long enough."[1] But Alice in Pleasant Valley set her feet in a definite direction, not just to anywhere. She knew what she wanted to do and where she wanted to go. Off she set — first to Mount Holyoke Female Seminary, and five years later to begin her own Select School at Berwick in Nova Scotia.

We first go back over twenty years to when the time was right, and so was the location. The time was the first day of spring — June 21st — a delightful period of the year, full of promise. And the place was well named as Pleasant Valley. In 1832, in Kings County, Nova Scotia, a baby girl Alice T. Shaw, entered the world. She was the daughter of Isaiah Shaw and Sarah Lyons; her grandfather was David Shaw whose father

124

was born in Barnstable, Massachusetts, and came to Granville, Nova Scotia, in the 1760's.[2] David was born in 1770 and the family moved to Pleasant Valley about 1810.[3] Alice's mother was descended from Charles Skinner who had first settled in New Brunswick before the Loyalists arrived. He left after the Loyalists settled, coming to the Cornwallis area of Kings County, Nova Scotia.[4]

Alice lived a long life, but never with her middle name publicized in any writings by or about her. She often wrote the complete names of her acquaintances, but Alice never disclosed the meaning of the letter "T." The name was Theodosia. But there was no mystery about her convictions, her attitude to life. She was decidedly an individualist who wished to be respected, and she maintained principles which she declared openly as worthy of honor and regard.

The earliest recorded incident about Alice revealed the nature of this young lady when she had not yet reached her sixth birthday. In her rural community of scattered houses, thinly spaced among the groves of mixed woods, a schoolhouse served the young children. Twenty-one year old Samuel Elder had charge of the Pleasant Valley School in 1838. The Pleasant Valley Baptist pastor, the Rev. William Chipman, converted Samuel; this experience changed him from "a confirmed Universalist" to a Baptist minister after his education at nearby Acadia College.[5]

It was said of him that he wrote valuable papers and "was passionately fond of children." Samuel Elder composed serious verses about Sin and Death. He had written a long poem on this theme to Alice, and he kissed her. She was less than six years old, but "this made me very angry," wrote Alice later.[6] Obviously, our Alice had a firm idea of what was right and wrong for her. She also developed a strong sense of what was right and wrong educationally for females of her generation.

How excited must have been the youngsters to gather in the schoolhouse in the 1840's. On one side of the room were an open fireplace and a teacher's desk. A shelf and a wide slanting board extended from the walls of the other three sides. The pupils sat facing the walls on "seats made of slabs supported by

125

legs made of stakes driven into auger holes." Later, a long continuous desk in sections and with covers improved the earlier arrangement. A stove stood now in the center of the room.[7]

Alice was baptized at the age of seventeen, a serious decision for her. She became a conscientious church member.[8] Alice's schooling and her Christian convictions encouraged her to write many poems about the world of nature, the joys of family relationships, and about her firm adherence to religious beliefs and moral values. God and eternity were real for her.[9]

That same family and religious background stimulated the desire for further education. From the Baptist parsonage and from her peers she got encouragement that sent her from Nova Scotia to a female seminary in Massachusetts.

II ALICE AND FEMALE SEMINARIES

Mary Lyon was in some respects similar in outlook to Alice. Mary was aged thirty-five when Alice was born. The result of Mary's considerable vision, energy and persistence was Mount Holyoke Female Seminary in Massachusetts. At South Hadley, girls received a three-year education in advanced subjects and deportment. The girls also did the housekeeping and cooking. This domestic plan meant for them a comparatively inexpensive course of study and training.[10]

The Rev. William Chipman and his son Isaac, who was professor at Acadia College, made available the printed life story of Mary Lyon to Alice and to other girls in that part of Nova Scotia. As a result, Alice, along with Annie Parker of Berwick and Rebecca Chase of Wolfville, decided that their only chance for further education was to go elsewhere, and they agreed on Mount Holyoke.[11] In 1854 they departed, perhaps by sailing vessel from Wolfville or by stage-coach to Halifax to take a steamer to Boston. They were accompanied by the Rev. John Chase, Rebecca's father. He later would begin a girls' school at Wolfville.

126

The three girls were the only non-Americans of that first-year class of one hundred sixty-two pupils. They brought their own towels and bedding, and one table spoon or dessert spoon, and "one spoon to be used by the family." Mary Lyon had established a family set-up which required punctuality and an hour-duty of domestic service. Rules were strict. For example, "The young ladies do not make or receive calls on the Sabbath." That is, observe the Sabbath for moral improvement and do it right at the Seminary.[12]

Despite the careful scheduling and the restrictions, Alice loved her Mount Holyoke experience and felt that Nova Scotia should have a Mount Holyoke-type of female seminary. She and other Nova Scotia graduates of Mount Holyoke set up similar schools when they returned home. One of these schools was established at Berwick by Miss Anna Fields, a native of New York and a graduate of Mount Holyoke in 1855. The three Nova Scotia girls had suggested the idea, and the Rev. John Chase encouraged her.[13]

Miss Field's Berwick Seminary was similar to several others established in various communities. The New Brunswick Baptists had founded in 1836 a co-educational Academy or Seminary at Fredericton,[14] but most of the Nova Scotia seminaries were solely for girls and young ladies. Acadia had Horton Academy for boys and young men, established 1828, but the Nova Scotia Baptist Education Society gave little thought to educating girls. Private community schools provided training not yet available from the provincial educational system. These female seminaries have been described as "of a very mild type, being chiefly devoted to 'deportment' and art studies in Berlin wool, with piano music and lead pencil drawing."[15] There were also female schools at Saint John, New Brunswick.

In the period from about 1835 to 1875 the female schools in Nova Scotia were to be found at Halifax, Liverpool, Clarence, Nictaux, Pine Grove or Wilmot, Middleton, Greenwich, Wolfville, Canning, Hantsport, Amherst, Sackville and Arichat. The Sackville Ladies College was Methodist, and that at Arichat was Roman Catholic. The Episcopalians came later. Beginning in the 1860's, a few of

127

these schools allowed boys and men to attend classes. One of the earliest schools for girls was run by a Mrs. Best at Wolfville, established about 1835 in what is now the Randall House Museum.[16]

Miss Field's Berwick Seminary started in 1855 in a dwelling house and hall and lasted one year. She had thirty-nine pupils and an establishment which the Rev. William Chipman and his community agreed was greatly needed to provide for female education. They even contemplated erecting a building there for that purpose.[17]

Now followed an uncertain period as letters to the Baptist weekly, the *Christian Messenger,* recommended a constitution for the seminary-to-be. They proposed locations for the institution and generally agitated that action be taken to provide for female schooling. Practically all contributions were signed by pen-names. "Observer" recommended Hantsport as a location for the Seminary because "it has a beach, too, free from mud, that may be walked on by a lady with Prunella slippers without being soiled."[18] And "Fausta" acknowledged that "literary women might have disordered dress and dishevelled hair, but the humble would have orderly thoughts and disciplined minds."[19]

To fill the vacancy caused by the closing in 1856 of the Berwick Female Seminary the Rev. John Chase erected a large residence at Wolfville. His two daughters had graduated from Mount Holyoke and they taught at the school on Main Street opposite the present Baptist church, on the site where stood later the Acadia Hotel, the Royal Hotel, and Evangeline Inn.[20]

The course of instruction at Mr. Chase's school resembled that of Mount Holyoke, but at that time "A Father" wrote, "Send the girls to Horton. . .Let them and the boys go to the same school — and through College." —same building, same subjects, so that the educated women can teach their children. "It is stated on good authority that some of the greatest men of the past and present have had dunces for fathers, but that they have all of them had intelligent mothers." Yes. Let them eat together. They might be attracted to one another. The tides of the Bay of Fundy or the command of Joshua are like to those forces needed to suppress these emotions. "Out upon such nonsense," trying to keep boys and girls separated from one another!²¹

On the other hand, "Progress" advised caution. He reminded "Reform" that an amalgamation of the females with the young men of Horton "would be running a risk beyond the bounds of prudence."²² But "Reform" later lamented the situation which required the six daughters of the Horton Academy Principal to get their schooling elsewhere than right at the Academy which was only ten rods away. "Reform" pointed out the need "which it would be well for the Education Society to consider and meet."²³

III ALICE AND HER BERWICK SEMINARY

There was now great need for female schooling, but it was also a period of educational enlightenment. Alice Shaw returned from Massachusetts to start in 1859 her Select School for young Ladies. She began at Berwick with six pupils and agreed with the local school to include only those over fourteen years of age.²⁴

Alice had a busy program that included "The School Quarterly," to which pupils contributed their writings. One described the Temperance Hall in Berwick "whose walls are not only the nursery of temperance principles, but in many ways occupies an important position in the intellectual and moral improvement of the inhabitants. This is a place for Temperance, social prayer and praise, and the Singing School."²⁵

The pages of the *Christian Messenger* were again alive with letters and editorials. The number of pupils at Alice's Select School reached a high of about forty, but the Baptist leaders were looking beyond her school at Berwick to a Baptist denominational Seminary, and they favored Wolfville for its location. Alice knew of this through her pastor, Rev. Mr. Chipman. So, late in 1860 she wrote to her good friend Alfred Chipman, the minister's son. He had graduated from the Academy, the College, and was now studying at Newton Theological Seminary in Massachusetts. She was excited, but somewhat fearful of such a responsibility in such a place as

Wolfville. "Pray that I might have wisdom to lead aright. Anew will I seek to give up myself and all my interests to God's keeping."[26]

The school at Berwick held its final closing. "The huge black-board was wheeled round," and a few girls did Algebra. Fifty-year old Silas Rand had difficulty recognizing some of the words of the singers who were unclear in their enunciation. But he was able to follow the "Doxology" and "Excelsior." He concluded, "We want a Female Academy on a large and more permanent scale — one that shall endure forever."[27] He got his wish. Alice decided to move from Berwick to Wolfville, to begin a Baptist Denomination Female Seminary there.

IV ALICE AND HER GRAND PRE SEMINARY

Alice now had charge of her own Baptist school. The possibilities for a superior educational program and for a larger number of pupils were great. Twenty of her pupils came with her.[28] The Education Society had rented the large house built by the Rev. John Chase,[29] and this the girls occupied. Soon the Seminary had fifty pupils.

The authorities revealed why Miss Shaw, "who had already advertised for another quarter at Berwick, should so suddenly change her plans." The reasons were lack of sufficient living accommodations and the need for more space for Music and Drawing. The girls themselves had encouraged the move because they considered that the Berwick Select School had limited prospects.[30]

In June of 1861 the Baptist Education Society reported real pleasure in the Female Department of Horton Academy — its location and its principal, Miss Shaw. They also commended themselves that they had Frank Higgins as Principal of the Academy and R. V. Jones and H. C. Creed as teachers.[31] The students would be able to attend some of the Academy classes, and the teachers of the Academy would devote part of their time to the female classes. The girls joined the Academy classes for Latin, French, Natural Philosophy, Chemistry and Mathematics.[32]

After June of 1861 the Horton Female Department acquired a new and distinctive name. One of the pupils had the idea. Irene Elder Morton recalled the memorable scene. "One day standing with our principal, Miss Shaw, at a high window which overlooked the green dykes of Grand Pre, the writer proposed to call our school 'Grand Pre Seminary.' "[33]Why not? Mary Lyon had named her Seminary Mount Holyoke after a nearby mountain.[34] How suitable to choose historic Grand Pre as a name for the Wolfville Baptist Seminary.

This was a happy school, with the pupils there for serious study, not just for "larks." Mount Holyoke Seminary had designed the pattern for the entire establishment. Alice had learned well from her experiences and she applied faithfully these teachings. Each pupil had an hour of domestic work, without missing any classes. This meant rising at five o'clock on a cold winter day, breaking the ice to get water to make porridge, hot rolls and coffee. Breakfast at 6.30. "No light but a smoky lamp. Each room had a small stove, and the girls took turns making the fires. Before going to breakfast, they filled the stoves. After eating and prayers, the stove and pipe were red hot. But never was there a happier lot of girls."[35]

Probably these girls at Grand Pre Seminary realized that they were pioneers as they now studied the same lessons and used the same books and teachers as did the boys. This contrasted with the general attitude toward females and education. Not until the 1890's did certain Baptists in the United States allow women the right to speak and to vote in their churches. Because females were considered inferior and weaker mentally, they were denied education. Girls were not allowed to assemblies attended by teenage boys.[36] Also there were English Baptists who hestitated to place women at the same level as man "who is the image and glory of God."[37]

Secular journalists told the same story of male reluctance to grant equality to females. Wrote one, "Even male sympathizers . . . may be glad in their own hearts that she is not their own wife or daughter."[38] Education could apparently be used for varying purposes. In 1857 an English writer concluded his argument, "I have great respect for the young lady who, being desperately in love, and having to give up her lover, went through the first four books of Euclid that she might not think of him."[39] A Canadian writer protested woman's rights to enter a military academy. "She has no more right to do this than she had to thrust her parasol through a picture in a public gallery."[40]

Back in Nova Scotia, the religious and secular writers were likewise hesitant, but more and more frequently the friends of female education voiced their support. Baptist support began as early as 1849. One spokesman then pictured the movement. It was hoped "to rear a structure, and assemble a company of instructors, whose impulsion of the female mind of this country shall not cease to perpetuate itself till time shall end, or ever."[41]

Alice Shaw and Grand Pre Seminary helped create the atmosphere which deposed the old attitude and introduced the new. The Rev. E.M. Saunders, Baptist historian, described the change.

> It was an epoch in the field of female education. The old sentiment received a death blow. It was not the dawn alone of a new and bright day; but the rising of the sun as well. It was a Spartan victory. These five young women[42] covered themselves with honor. Their names will go down to posterity as the little band who reversed the current of public sentiment, and turned it into a new channel.[43]

Alice Shaw and her contemporaries sensed the strain and heard utterances that perplexed them. The Academy principal gave them hope. "I look forward to the day when our girls as well as our boys shall graduate from our College platform."[44] Irene Elder gasped at such a bold idea, and wrote her reaction: "I remember the ominous shake of the head of a venerable D.D. of conservative tendencies, who sat upon the platform." As late as about 1880, and with some misgiving, the College president gave the Seminary girls permission to attend classes at the College, but "You must not consider yourselves as members of the College, young ladies."[45]

From the student point of view the serious matter was regarded in a different light. One óf the young male teachers recalled, "In January, 1861, the girls began to flit about 'The Great House in the Village' . . . These were days of romance, — of trembling hearts, — of sunny smiles, — of high hopes, — of youthful fancies. Happy days! Let our poets tell of them, not the prosaic secretary."[46]

V GRAND PRE SEMINARY ACTIVITIES

Nova Scotia Baptists began Grand Pre Seminary, as the fathers of the denomination had already begun Horton Academy and Acadia College. These early years were marked by a religious emphasis which made Christian dedication a fundamental criterion for a righteous life. Regularly, revival services were held, and the preachers challenged all students to commit themselves to follow Christ. Few were already declared Christians and church members.

Alice Shaw led a Sabbath afternoon prayer meeting. Girls, with tears flowing, testified to their new-found faith, and nine of them were baptized in the Gaspereau River by the Wolfville pastor, the Rev. Stephen DeBlois.[47] At other times, the girls enjoyed the Sunday evening sing, the parlor prayer meetings and Bible lessons, the late evening prayer circles in their rooms, and weekly prayer and conference meetings. But the most satisfying occasion was the annual revival which was looked forward to as much as the Christmas vacation.[48]

This early group of pupils enjoyed social activities as well. Alice and the Academy principal and "a party of eight couples — Collegians and some of their friends, drove by waggon to Black River — about six or seven miles for an outing."[49] The freedom allowed at this time by Alice and her school is surprising. However, a Seminary student recalled the social life differently. "In the old times a social once a year was considered sufficient, and such a thing as going on sleigh drives, midnight suppers, and Banquets were never thought of."[50]

Life was simpler then, with little noise pollution to disturb the peace. No college yells or medals or colors. No railway to Wolfville, only stage-coaches. "And some of us who were sentimental thought it would be a desecration of the sacred precincts to let the puffing, screaming iron horse invade them." Group sports for boys was limited to cricket. " 'Muscular Christianity' had scarcely then begun its propaganda."[51]

The College, Academy and Seminary joined in a literary activity. Together, they produced and published *The Academy Budget*. The handwritten paper of four and six pages was a large sheet of thick paper, with the headings stamped out by a small lettering set. Only two copies were made each time.

The serious-minded contributors echoed the editor's ambition to "think, write, live *earnestly*."[52] The paper employed a group of pupils who planned and worked together amicably and with good effect. But a controversy about the boys loitering on Sabbath evenings outside the Meeting House caused a division. According to the female writers, the boys were over-zealous in their attempts to walk the girls home from the church meetings to their "Great House in the Village." Both male and female writers made sharp comments against one another.[53] And the new principal, who followed Alice Shaw in the summer of 1862, questioned the propriety of males and females working so closely together. All this led to the paper's demise. One student expressed in verse the annoyance at this unsatisfying conclusion.

> "Toll for the fair,
> Whose charms we see no more
> Except as pair by pair
> They pass the College door."[54]

VI   ALICE AND GRAND PRE SEMINARY BOW OUT

Due to ill health, Alice left her responsible position as principal of Grand Pre Seminary after a year and half of service. The Baptist Education Society praised her for her ability as her services were highly esteemed.[55] Alice's sister Annie graduated from the Seminary. The friends of the Seminary rejoiced at this. "Those who have fought so bravely and so long for an 'Institution for female education' hailed this event with great delight. It was the dawn of a new day."[56]

Grand Pre Seminary continued by that name for another ten years. Female seminaries had become numerous. Also, the provincial educational system increasingly provided more convenient study oportunities for girls of high school age. Still, through the *Christian Messenger,* several believers in female education advocated a larger and better building. Letter after letter, year after year stressed this theme, but nothing happened — no building.

However, changes did take place in administration. An unsettling event occurred when Grand Pre Seminary closed in 1870 because of lowered attendance and insufficient funds. For two years the school was located at Pine Grove, near Middleton, with Miss M. R. Eaton giving voluntary teaching leadership. She had an earnest concern for continued female education.[57] When the "Great House in the Village" was sold in 1870, the Baptist Education Society conveyed the ownership of the furniture to the Governors of Acadia College, and the College also purchased the property.[58]

Another change took place. When the school began again at Wolfville in 1872, this time as the Female Department of Horton Academy, the senior girls attended some of the Academy classes. This was the opening wedge. "In 1873, the Seminary came to the Hill" and was conducted on the Acadia Campus, all the classes open to female pupils.[59]

This development should have meant a state of victory and satisfaction. Had not the Seminary girls been admitted to the classes with the boys? Unfortunately, the living accommodations were still too limited and cramped. The girls needed a building of their own, as did the boys of the Academy. In 1876 the girls even petitioned the Governors that a building be reserved for them in any future plans.[60] The Governors tried to meet the need. A large boarding house was erected for girls on the Campus, and in 1877 a new boys Academy building opened.[61]

Then disaster struck on Dec. 5, 1877. The Acadia College building burned to the ground.[62] Lost were class rooms, part of the library, and all of the museum. The students later "formed themselves into a procession with mounted marshall, and solemnly marched twice round the ruins, singing 'Auld Lang Syne.' "[63]

But a new note sounded as the friends of Acadia considered the future. One of them wrote; "The way seems to be opened, and there is a fair prospect that a building will be erected in which the young ladies will be well cared for, physically, mentally, morally."[64] The College Hall was replaced, and for the fall term of 1879, just one hundred years ago, the new Seminary was completed and opened for a residence and classes.[65] The old wooden building still stands in this historic centennial year.

VII VICTORY FOR ALICE AND FEMALE EDUCATION

The battle for female education was won at last. Persistence, with an assist from a fateful or providential fire, finally gained for the young ladies their place on the campus in which to live and study. Five years after the new Seminary opened, in 1884, Acadia College graduated its first female. Clara Marshall, (Mrs. E. W. Raymond), holds that distinction. "Since 1893, no class of Acadia has graduated without at least one woman among the graduates."[66]

Grand Pre Seminary and its eleven years of existence under that name was a watershed. The rocky hillside of doubt and struggle marked the difficult progress toward educational enlightenment. On this side of that high point the way has sloped more gently as disagreeable conflict lessened and as society finally recognized the educational rights of females. Toward the end of the nineteenth century girls could procure an education equal to that of boys.

In these years, girls like Alice Shaw, Irene Elder, Anna D. Shaw, Rosina Bently gave Grand Pre Seminary a personality of a distinctive quality. Irene Elder Morton wrote in 1905, "We rejoice that the light of the Seminary grows brighter . . . From our school may there continue to flow the best and holiest influence into the sacred portals of Canadian Homes.[67]

What of Alice Shaw? Alice's husband, Alfred Chipman, was ordained in the fall of 1862, a month after his
136

marriage to Alice in October. Three boys were born in 1865, 1867, and 1871. She and Alfred labored together in several small churches, some of them home mission churches.[68] She wrote occasionally to her beloved Mount Holyoke Seminary.[69] When she wrote for an Acadia Seminary anniversary celebration in 1892 she recalled her "loved pupils of '59 to '62," especially the twenty who encouraged her to move from Berwick to Wolfville.[70]

Then came retirement for Alfred to Berwick in 1899. He received an honorary Doctorate of Divinity from Acadia College in 1912. Acadia Seminary honored Alice in 1912 with a painting of her presented to the Seminary and with a certificate of membership in the Alumnae Society. She gave an address at that Jubilee celebration.[71] In 1915 she responded to a questionaire from Mount Holyoke and told them with pride that "she had taken first prize, $15.00, in artistic arrangement of fruit, in Provincial Exhibition, when in 83rd year of age."[72]

Life ended for Alfred in 1918 at the age of 84. Alice T. Shaw Chipman died in January, 1921, at the age of 88. The Baptist Convention reported of Alice, "Her life was one of great devotion to God and the work of His Kingdom."[73]

> Our Home is there. We sojourn here but for a little day,
> That we may prove our Saviour's love and His blest will obey.
> It matters not how soon we go or how long we stay,
> If we are but prepared to hear, 'My loved one, come away.'[74]

The Union of the Regular
and Free Will Baptists
of the Maritimes, 1905 and 1906

F. H. SINNOTT

In any history of the union of the two Maritime Baptist bodies in the first decade of the twentieth century one has to look back to the origin of the Baptist movement on the continent of Europe and the British Isles, back to the Reformation and even beyond.

Dr. J.K. Zeman in his recent book *Baptist Roots and Identity* traces these origins back to the continental Anabaptist movement and English Separatism during the sixteenth and seventeenth centuries.[1] The springing up of many new groups, or denominations, as they were later called, — namely, Lutherans, Calvinists, Methodists, Puritans, Congregationalists and Baptists, among others — is due to several events which occurred as a result of the transition of the western world out of the "Middle Ages" to the "Modern Period." The invention of printing (1424-1448), the revival of learning, the religious revolution (the Reformation), combined to set the western world on a new course which culminated in the founding of the American colonies, the rise of democracy, religious freedom, the separation of Church and State and the two Great Awakenings or revivals in the United States. All of these movements contributed to the rise of the Baptist Denomination.[2]

138

Beginning with Roger Williams, the first Baptists in the New England Colonies were Calvinists in theology; they brought their Calvinist heritage with them from England, Scotland and the continent of Europe. Gradually the harsh Calvinistic views were softened by the circumstances of life which existed in New England in those challenging times.

Among the strong influences which helped to soften the harsh Calvinistic views was the rise of the Free Will Baptists, who according to Norman Baxter "reflected the mood of protest then arising against the Calvinism then prevailing in New England."[3]

The Free Will Baptist Denomination began in New England with the conversion of Benjamin Randall (1780-1808). Randall saw in his conversion experience "a universal love, a universal atonement, a universal call to mankind, and was confident that none would ever perish but those who refused to obey it."[4] This is in exact contrast to the doctrines of election and limited atonement of Calvinism.

In Dr. George Levy's history, *The Baptists of the Maritime Provinces,* he refers to the earliest known groups in the Maritime region to subscribe to beliefs essentially Baptist. These newcomers formed part of the stream of Protestant migration, mostly German, but with a sprinkling of French and Swiss, that flowed in the early 1750s to Halifax and later to what is known as Lunenburg County.[5] The Rev. Ebenezer Moulton of Brimfield, Mass., is recognized as the first of the New England Baptists to come to Nova Scotia, arriving at Chebogue in Yarmouth County. He came in the year 1760, and did some work in the Yarmouth area and at Horton, N.S.[6] He was followed in the same year by the Alline family, who moved from New England to the Falmouth region. Henry Alline was converted at Falmouth in 1775 and began to preach the next year. Alline was brought up a Congregationalist but after his conversion diverged more and more from the basic Calvinism of the Congregationalist Church. He sparked a revival of religion in the Annapolis Valley and other parts of the Maritime region; out of this revival many Baptist Churches were eventually founded.

A group of Baptists of New England from the town of Swansea, Mass., organized themselves into a Baptist Church while still in Swansea, then migrated to Sackville, in presentday New Brunswick. Here, in 1763, they established the first Baptist Church in what is now Canada, but because of unfavourable conditions in the area most of the settlers returned to New England in 1771. The Church lapsed and was not reconstituted until nearly thirty years later.[7]

The oldest continuing Baptist Church in Canada was founded at Horton, now Wolfville, N.S. in 1765. Lack of leadership and falling support apparently caused the church's disintegration; it was recovenanted in 1778 as the result of Alline's revival.[8]

The Free Will Baptists cannot pinpoint the exact time their work began in New Brunswick, but the body which became known as the Free Baptist General Conference was organized at Wakefield, Carleton Co., N.B., on October 13, 1832.[9] Similar developments were taking place in nearby Nova Scotia at much the same time. For both of these movements, much of the early Free Will influence came from the State of Maine.

Both the Regular (or Calvinistic) and the Free Will Baptist bodies grew rapidly as the population of the Maritimes expanded until by 1884 there were two fairly large groups similar in doctrine and practice working side by side in the region. As time passed, earlier differences blurred, inevitably drawing the two groups together.

During the middle years of the nineteenth century there were at least two influences which made both the Regular Baptists and the Free Christian Baptists consider the question of closer union within their respective groups, a necessary prelude to the larger union. In the first place the Regular Baptists of the Maritimes were approached in 1846 to consider seriously the possibility of a closer relationship between the Regular Baptists of the Maritimes and all other Baptists in British North America (present-day Canada). It was not until 100 years later that such a union came about. The minutes of the Nova Scotia Association disclose the following:

140

A letter from the Canada Baptist Union to the Nova Scotia Baptist Association having been read, expressing the desirability of a closer union between all the Baptists of British North America being effected and manifested, and declaring the Rev. Mr. Cramp to be representative of such a union at their session of Association. It was resolved that Rev. Dr. Crawley, Rev. W. Chipman, and R.B. Dickey, be a committee to meet Bro. Cramp and confer with him on the object of his mission.[10]

This approach is significant for it expresses the wide-spread interest in the union of the Baptist bodies during this period.

The Baptist people of British North America found that their denominations had grown rapidly and that some larger union was now needed which would help them all work more efficiently. The call to a larger unity helped spur on the contemplated union of Regular Baptists of New Brunswick, Nova Scotia and Prince Edward Island into a Convention, a task which was finally accomplished in the same year, 1846.[11]

From this time forward, Baptists in British North America/Canada never quite lost the vision of the union of all Baptist bodies in the country. It is interesting to note that when the two main Baptist bodies in the Maritime Provinces (Regular and Free Will) talked about uniting, they did not limit their discussions to themselves, but included the Primitive Baptists and the Reformed Baptists in their plans for organic union of all Baptists in the region.

The first real step toward such an organic union was taken in 1884, twenty-one years before the actual union of these two bodies.[12] In October, 1884, the Free Baptist Conference of New Brunswick was held in Fredericton, N.B. To this meeting came a delegation from the Baptist Convention of the Maritime Provinces, with instructions to purpose that the denominations co-operate in foreign mission work. The Free Baptist Conference did not regard the proposition with favor. Instead, it intimated a willingness to consider the broader question of the organic union of the denominations. This matter was reported to the Baptist Convention at its next session (1885). The Covention adopted a resolution warmly endorsing the union proposal.[13]

The Free Baptist Conference of 1886 received a delegation from the Baptist Convention, which presented the greetings of the Baptists and expressed their desire for union. The Conference reciprocated the sentiments of their Baptist brethren, and appointed a delegation to Convention instructing them to say that the Conference was prepared to appoint its part of a joint Committee to canvass the whole question, and if possible, suggest a general basis of union of the two bodies.[14]

The Conference of 1886 received a communication from the Baptist Convention saying that the Convention had appointed a committeee to consider with a committee of the Conference the question of union, and to endeavor to frame a basis of union. Responding to this action of the Convention, the Conference adopted this resolution:

> That we have heard with pleasure the desire of the Convention for the union of the Baptists and the Free Baptists of the Maritime Provinces, that we heartily reciprocate the desire and shall rejoice, if it be the will of God, that such a union should be consummated.[15]

A committee of fifteen men was appointed to draft a basis of union. The Conference also recommended that the Reverends E. Crowell and S.N. Royal of the Nova Scotia Free Baptist Conference, who were present, be requested to meet with the joint committee in the expectation that if the union should be effected the Free Baptists of Nova Scotia would also join in the union.[16]

The joint committee met in Saint John on October 14 and 15, 1886. The whole question of union was thoroughly discussed with much prayer for guidance. The articles of faith and policy of the denominations were closely examined and all the interests involved were given due consideration. A sub-committee was appointed to further examine the doctrinal

142

statements and arrange a basis of agreement which was approved and adopted by the full joint committee.[17]

The Baptist Convention held at Charlottetown, P.E.I., in August, 1887, adopted the proposed basis of union. It then appeared the union might very soon be accomplished. But the Free Baptist Conference held in October, 1887, decided to defer action. The deferment was caused by internal trouble within the Free Baptist Conference, culminating in the secession of several churches.[18] The internal trouble referred to had to do with several Free Christian Baptist pastors who embraced the doctrine of 'Instantaneous Sanctification', a doctrine which the majority of Free Christian Baptists could not condone. The result of this doctrinal controversy was that those who believed this radical doctrine were either dismissed or withdrew from the fellowship. Until this matter was settled the Free Christian Baptists could not talk union with the Regular Baptists.[19]

During the interval there were frequent fraternal communications between the Convention and the Conference by delegation and otherwise, but definite negotiations for organic union were discontinued.[20]

In 1889 there were signs in the Free Baptist Conference of a desire to take up the question of organic union again. The feeling grew quietly and steadily. The Baptist Convention was aware of it, and in the session of 1903 adopted a resolution favoring the reopening of negotiations and appointed a committee to meet a like committee of the Free Baptist Conference to again consider the question. The Conference in session in October, 1903, considered the original basis of union and adopted it with slight modifications in two sections, and also appointed a committee to meet with the Regular Baptist Committee.[21]

The amendments to the Basis of Union proposed by the Free Baptist Conference were these: (1) That clause II of the basis of union be dropped out. (2) That clause 16 read: The Lord's Supper — We believe that the Lord's Supper is an ordinance of Christ, to be observed by the Churches in accordance with His instructions. (Matt. 26:26-30) (This is a very clear and simple statement, leaving it to the Churches to

143

conduct it according to their understanding of the New Testament teaching.) A motion to adopt the Basis of Union with the foregoing amendments was then carried unanimously.[22]

These committees in joint session followed a path of organization which with the Basis as amended by the Conference was presented to the Convention congregations. That body voted approval but made other slight changes in the statement of doctrinal beliefs. The changes, in both cases, were with a view of the avoidance of possible misunderstandings and to afford the truest liberty for all.[23]

Dr. G.O. Gates was the leader in the Baptist Convention in all the negotiations for union of the two bodies. It was Gates who headed the committee of the Baptist Convention which actually formulated the articles of the Basis of Union and the policy that underlay that document. In his discussions on the subject of union, he deplored the fact that there were two large bodies of Baptists with practically the same doctrinal teaching, living side by side, working in the same field, with the same outreach, and yet not united. He recognized the waste of money in duplication of effort, and was thrilled that the two bodies could get together and in the Lord be one. In 1904, at the Baptist Convention, at Truro the following report was presented:

> It was the unanimous expression of the joint-committee that the union of the Baptist bodies there represented is a very remarkable thing, desirable because united we could do more for the Kingdom, and would enable us to show the world the Spirit of the Master in His prayer on the eve of His passion 'that they all may be one.'[24]

The Conference is session of September, 1904, adopted the amended Basis of Union and approved the plan of organization. The matter was referred to the churches for their concurrence. A committee was authorized, in the event of ratification of the Conference action by the churches, to take steps to consummate the union. The churches with remarkable unanimity voted approval of the Basis adopted by the
144

Convention. The committee pursuant to instructions in joint-meeting with the Baptist Committee, on April 4, 1905, made the final arrangements for the proclamation of this union which took place on that same day.[25]

The meeting for the formal uniting of the Baptist and Free Baptist bodies was held in the Main Street Baptist Church, Saint John, on Tuesday evening, October 10, 1905, before a capacity audience. The next morning Oct. 11, there appeared in the Saint John *Daily Sun* the following bold headlines:

Baptists and Free Baptists are United. Impréssive and spectacular ceremony in Main Street Baptist Church last evening. Big edifice packed to the doors. Service one long to be remembered.

Rev. David Hutchinson was the pastor of the Main Street Church at the time.[26]

As President of the Baptist Convention of the Maritime Provinces, I now declare the union of the Baptists of the Maritime Provinces and the Free Baptists of New Brunswick as consummated.

It now becomes my duty as president of the Free Baptist Conference of New Brunswick on behalf of the Conference, to declare the union of the Baptists of the Maritime Provinces and the Free Baptists of New Brunswick is now consummated, and may God bless the union.[27]

Thus solemnly did the Rev. George R. White and Dr. Joseph McLeod on behalf of these two large denominations declare their union, as with upraised hands they advanced to the pulpit and made formal announcement of the consummation of a work that for the past 21 years had occupied the minds and hearts of men representing a body of many thousands of Christian worshippers.

In 1906 the Free Baptists of Nova Scotia joined the new United Baptist Convention, thus making the union complete.[28] There were in 1906 as a result of this union over 61,000 Baptists in one organization in these Maritime Provinces. Throughout the past 70 years or more we have held our own, but that is all.

We are at about the same numerical strength now as we were at the time of the union, and that in the face of a great increase in population in these same provinces.[29]

Saunders began his *History of the Baptists of the Maritime Provinces* with the following paragraph, which serves as a fitting summation of the feelings which helped bring together the Baptists of this region:

> The principles peculiar to Baptists can be traced in the history of the Christian Religion from the Apostolic age till the present day. There is not, it is true, a clear succession of Churches of the New Testament model, but the doctrines of a regenerate Church membership, of believers' baptism by immersion as the only scriptual mode, of the independent self-government of each church, and of the two distinct spheres of Church and State, appear from time to time, and can be traced along the whole course of the history of the Christian religion. These principles have been irrepressible. They have passed through the floods of persecution and of martyrdom.[30]

It was the realization of the importance of these shared principles that, breaking down the barriers of the past, led to the achievement of union in 1905-06.

The Rev. Joseph McLeod, D. D.

Joseph McLeod was the son of the Rev. Ezekiel McLeod, an outstanding minister of the Free Baptist Conference in New Brunswick. Joseph McLeod was born in Saint John, N.B., June 27, 1844. He was converted in early life, and in 1868 was ordained to the Gospel Ministry. He became pastor of the George Street Free Baptist Church, Fredericton, N.B., succeeding his illustrious father. This, his only pastorate, continued for 26 years., For forty-seven years he served as editor of denominational papers. From 1866 to 1905 he was editor and publisher of the *Christian Intelligencer,* the organ of the Free Baptist Conference of New Brunswick. When in 1905 the *Messenger and Visitor* and the *Religious Intelligencer* were united, Dr. McLeod became associate editor along with the late S. McCully Black, D.D., and when in 1909 Dr. Black was called higher, Dr. McLeod became the sole editor and so continued until his death. Such was the great life work of Dr. McLeod. But there were other and more incidental services. For eighteen consecutive years he was Chaplain of the Legislative Assembly at Fredericton. He was a member of the Royal Commission of Canada appointed by the Dominion Government to investigate the liquor problem and to inquire into the working of Prohibition. Here he rendered splendid service. He represented the Maritime Baptists at the First (World) Baptist Congress in London. After 1907 he served as a member of the Board of Governors of Acadia University. He was a member of the Dominion Board of Foreign Missions.[31]

A noteworthy feature of the Maritime Free Baptist history during the later period was the Conference Jubilees. The N.B. Free Christian Baptists celebrated their 50th anniversary at the scene of the formation of the original Conference — Wakefield, Victoria Corner, Carleton Co., September, 1882. The Rev. Joseph McLeod presented an historical sketch entitled, 'The Rise and Progress of the Denomination'. Those assembled manifested due pride in the growth of their denomination. The beginnings had been small, but according to the Dominion Statistics of 1881, there were in the province 31,603 adherents, of whom 10,529 were communicants. The attendance at the Jubilee observance was unusually large.

Although a spirit of unity was apparent at each Jubilee observance, a deep undercurrent of dissension was beginning to disturb the peace of both the Nova Scotia and New Brunswick Conferences. A heated controversy over the doctrine of Holiness was soon precipitated and led eventually to the formation of the "Primitive" and "Reformed" Baptist bodies. During the same period the Conferences made a number of changes in their administrative machinery in the hope of promoting greater efficiency. But as the century neared its close one matter of paramount importance claimed attention above all others — union with the Regular Baptists. Then, in 1905 and 1906, the decision was made which the events since have proven wise and significant — the formation of one denomination under the direction of the United Baptist Convention of the Maritime Provinces.[32]

Dr. McLeod served as the first President of the United Baptist Convention. He was a child of the public schools of New Brunswick and of the Baptist Seminary at Fredericton. In 1886 Acadia College conferred on him the honorary degree of Doctor of Divinity. Joseph McLeod was always an outstanding character. His large body surmounted by a massive head marked him at once as a leader of men. But it was his moral force which above all else constituted him as a leader. For many years he was easily first among his Free Baptist brethren. In the united body he was at once accepted as a leader. This was well, for he had done more than any other man to bring about the union. His whole soul went into this movement because he saw it was of God.

His long period of service as editor has left its impression upon the life of these provinces. But it is as a great moral reformer that Joseph McLeod stands amongst the foremost men of his generation. His was the soul of the reformer. He loved righteousness with all his might. He hated iniquity with every power of his personality. He was an intense lover and a great hater. Such men develp intense friendships and make bitter opponents. Such was the lot of Dr. McLeod. But Joseph McLeod was more than a reformer. He was a former. His was the vision of a Christian statesman. His vision took in the immense sweep of the interests of the Kingdom of God throughout Canada and he burned with a passion for an organization including all the Baptist Churches from the Atlantic to the Pacific. He saw in the Canada of today the great nation of tomorrow, playing her part, and a great part, in the development of the Empire. He consistently called upon the Baptists of Canada to close up their scattered ranks that
148

they might be prepared for the herculean task which McLeod believed lay before them.[33] •

He died in Saint John, N.B., June 24, 1913, at the age of 69.[34]

The Rev. George Oscar Gates, D.D.

George Oscar Gates was born in Melvern Square, N.S., Oct. 17, 1846. At the age of 18 he commenced teaching school. After a course at Horton Academy he entered Acadia College, where he took his B.A. in 1873, graduating at the head of his class. A few years later he took the M.A. Degree in Course. During his college course he did missionary work in Colchester County, also spending one summer as assistant to Dr. Steele in Amherst. In his senior year he supplied the Baptist Church in Gaspereaux. In the autumn of 1873, he was called to the pastorate of the Church in Liverpool, remaining there until June, 1880, when he went to the First Church at Moncton where he remained until the autumn of 1885. In January 1886, he went to Germain Street Church, Saint John, remaining for 15 years, after which he served in Windsor for nearly two years. Returning to the Germain St. Church he remained there nearly three years longer, when he went to Westmount, P.Q., in 1906, ending his pastorate there in 1913.[35]

Dr. Gates was a member of the Foreign Mission Board of the Baptist Convention of the Maritime Provinces, 1880-1906. He was a Senator of Acadia University 1891-1906. He was Secretary of the Committee on the Union of the Regular Baptists and Free Baptists in New Brunswick.

He spent his last years in Wolfville where he supplied the Baptist Church to a considerable extent. He died in Wolfville, January 1, 1923.

Dr. Gates had a large measure of success in the ministry. During one year at Moncton, one hundred and forty were added to the Church, and while there, there was a steady increase of members including a large number from the Sunday School. He always took a deep interest in Sunday School, missionary work and the Provincial Sunday School Association. He was also at one time President of the Grande

149

Ligne Mission, and President of the Sunday School Association of the Province of Quebec. In all his pastorates Dr. Gates proved himself an earnest and faithful worker.[36]

Gates, always an enthusiastic supporter of youth organizations, initiated a discussion of this work at the Convention of 1891. As a result of this consideration, a committee was named to plan the future of Young People's work in the Baptist Churches throughout the Convention, and to proceed with the organization of a B. Y. P. Convention at the main Convention at Bridgetown in August, 1892.[37]

One of the St. John papers referring to Dr. Gates said: "As a preacher he is unsurpassed by any in the city, and as a citizen his personal popularity extends far beyond the bounds of his Church and Denomination, and his departure will be keenly felt. "[38]

But perhaps his most outstanding contribution to the work of the Baptists of the Maritime Provinces was his leadership in the movement for the union of the two great bodies, the Regular Baptists and the Free Baptists. T.D. Denham, Germain Street Church historian, says that "a very large measure of credit in the progress of this movement is to be accorded to Dr. Gates who by his energetic and strenuous endeavors as Chairman of the Union Committee, representing the Baptists, may be said to have been greatly instrumental in consummating the union of these two branches of the one Body."[39]

It was under the leadership of men such as G.O. Gates that the Convention and the individual churches of the Regular Baptist movement were brought to contemplate union with the Free Baptists in 1905-06.

Notes
From New Light to Baptist:
Harris Harding and the Second Great Awakening
in Nova Scotia

1   J. Davis, *Life and Times of the Late Rev. Harris Harding* (Charlottetown,1866), p. 75.
2   W.G. McLoughlin, *Revivals, Awakenings and Reform* (Chicago, 1978).
3   See R. D. Shiels, "The Myth of the Second Great Awakening," (Paper delivered at the American Historical Association, Dec. 28, 1977); R. Birdsall "The Second Great Awakening and the New England Social Order," *Church History,* 39 (1970), pp. 345-364; S. Berk, *Calvinism Versus Democracy: Timothy Dwight and the Origins of American Evangelical Orthodoxy* (Hamden, 1974); McLoughlin, *Revivals, Awakenings and Reform,* pp. 98-140; N.O. Hatch, *The Sacred Cause of Liberty* (New Haven, 1977). For the Nova Scotia side, see M. Armstrong, *The Great Awakening in Nova Scotia, 1776-1809* (Hartford, 1948), pp. 119-138; S.D. Clark, *Church and Sect in Canada* (Toronto, 1948), pp. 45-89. An often overlooked but important study is G. E. Levy, *The Baptists of the Maritime Provinces 1753-1946* (Saint John, 1946), pp. 41-85.
4   M. W. Armstrong, "Neutrality and Religion in Revolutionary Nova Scotia," in G. A. Rawlyk (ed.), *Historical Essays on the Atlantic Provinces* (Toronto, 1967), p. 40
5   S. D. Clark, *Movements of Political Protest in Canada 1640-1840* (Toronto 1959), p. 7.

6   J. M. Bumsted, *Henry Alline* (Toronto, 1971), p. 68.

7   G. Stewart, "Religion and the Yankee Mind during the American Revolution" (Unpublished Ph.D. thesis, Queen's University, 1970); see also G. Stewart and G. A. Rawlyk, *A People Highly Favoured of God* (Toronto, 1972).

8   G. A. Rawlyk, "Henry Alline and the Canadian Baptist Tradition," McMaster Divinity College *Theological Bulletin,* Vol. IV (No. 4), (June, 1977), p. 4.

9   *Massachusetts Baptist Missionary Magazine,* 1808, pp. 303-305.

10 *Ibid,* pp. 305-307.

11 *Ibid,* p. 307.

12 *Ibid,* pp. 307-309.

13 *Ibid.*

14 Public Archives of Nova Scotia, Halifax, N.S. (hereafter P.A.N.S.), "The Journal of Mr. Reverend John Payzant... 1760-1810;" see also B. Cuthbertson, "The Reverend John Payzant: Henry Alline's Successor," (Paper presented in 1977 in Halifax, at the Nova Scotia Historical Society).

15 *Ibid.*

16 G.E. Levy (ed.), *The Diary of Joseph Dimock*(Hantsport, 1979), pp. 83-84.

17 I. E. Bill, *Fifty Years with the Baptist Ministers and Churches of the Maritime Provinces of Canada* (Saint John, 1880), pp. 201-202.

18 E. M. Saunders, *History of the Baptists of the Maritime Provinces* (Halifax, 1902), p. 93.

19 C. B. Fergusson (ed.), *The Diary of Simeon Perkins, 1790-1796,* p. 177; *Perkins' Diary, 1797-1803,* p. 18.

20 *Perkins' Diary, 1790-1796,* p. 428.

21 Davis, *Harris Harding,* p. 26.

22 *Ibid,* pp. 146-148.

23 T. S. Harding's "Recollections of Harris Harding," March 10, 1854, in Davis, *Harris Harding*, p. 168.

24 In Davis, *Harris Harding*, p. 153.

25 *Ibid.*, p. 74.

26 *Ibid.*, pp. 9-14.

27 P.A.N.S., "Payzant Journal".

28 Davis, *Harris Harding*, pp. 21-40.

29 *Ibid.*, p. 143.

30 *Ibid.*

31 *Perkins' Diary, 1790-1796,* p. 174.

32 Davis, *Harris Harding,* p. 33.

33 See H. Harding to D. Prentice, September 17, 1791, in Davis, *Harris Harding*, pp. 228-229 and H. Harding to T. Bennett, April 6, 1792, in *ibid.,* p. 231.

34 Quoted in Davis, *Harris Harding,* p. 224.

35 H. Harding to J. Payzant, August 23, 1791, quoted in *ibid*, p. 227.

36 H. Harding to T. Bennett, April 6, 1792, in *ibid.*, pp. 231-232.

37 Acadia University Archives (hereafter A.U.A.), Wolfville, N.S., Manning Papers.

38 A.U.A., Manning Papers, H. Harding to D. Prentice, August 27, 1791.

39 H. Harding to D. Prentice, September 17, 1791, in Davis, *Harris Harding,* p. 229.

40 A.U.A., H. Harding to W. Alline, April 6, 1792, in J.M. Cramp, "History of the Maritime Baptists," p. 33.

41 A.U.A., Manning Papers, H. Harding to D. Prentice, August 27, 1791.

42 Cramp, "History", p. 35.

43 P.A.N.S., "Payzant Journal."

44 Quoted in Cramp, "History", p. 24.

45 P.A.N.S., "Payzant Journal."

46 *Ibid.*

47 *Perkins' Diary, 1797-1803,* p. 45.

48 Levy, *Diary of Joseph Dimock,* p. 13.

49 P.A.N.S. "Payzant Journal;" Cramp, "History", p. 36.

50 *Ibid.*

51 Levy, *Baptists of the Maritime Provinces,* p. 52.

52 Cramp, "History", p. 75.

53 Saunders, *History of the Baptists,* p. 28.

54 *Ibid.,* p. 71.

55 Quoted in Cramp, "History", p. 73.

56 H. Harding, "Account of the Rise and Progress of the First Baptist Church in Yarmouth", quoted in Davis, *Harris Harding,* p. 206.

57 P.A.N.S., "Chebogue Church Records."

58 H. Harding to J. Dimock, January 27, 1792, in Davis, *Harris Harding,* p. 59; and H. Harding to T. Bennett, April 6, 1792, quoted in Cramp, "History", p. 33.

59 Quoted in Cramp, "History", p. 36.

60 *Perkins' Diary, 1790-1796,* p. 386.

61 *Ibid.,* p. 387.

62 A.U.A., Manning Papers, Mrs. D. Wright to T. Bennett, September 20, 1793.

63 P.A.N.S. "Payzant Journal."

64 *Ibid.*

65 *Perkins' Diary, 1797-1803,* p. 20.

66 Davis, *Harris Harding,* p. 73.

67 Cramp, "History", p. 73.

68 Quoted in *ibid.,* p. 73.

69 *Classified Digest of the Records of the Society for the Propagation of the Gospel in Foreign Parts, 1701-1892* (London, 1893), p. 118.

70 Quoted in Saunders, *History of the Baptists,* p. 115.
71 *Ibid.*
72 Cramp, "History", pp. 74-5.
73 Quoted in *ibid.,* p. 75.
74 *Ibid.*
75 P.A.N.S. "Payzant Journal."
76 *Ibid.*
77 Quoted in Cramp, "History", p. 75.
78 *Ibid.,* p. 76.
79 Quoted in *ibid.,* p. 76.
80 Quoted in *ibid.,* p. 92.
81 Davis, *Harris Harding,* p. 78.
82 J. Fingard, *The Anglican Design in Loyalist Nova Scotia, 1783-1816* (London, 1972), p. 60.
83 Quoted in Davis, *Harris Harding,* p. 79.
84 Quoted in *ibid.,* p. 23.
85 P. Miller, *Errand Into the Wilderness* (Cambridge, 1964), p. 167.
86 Davis, *Harris Harding,* p. 220.
87 *Ibid.*
88 *Ibid.,* pp. 217-218.
89 See W.J. Ong, *The Presence of the Word: Some Prolegomena for Cultural and Religious History* (New Haven, 1967).
90 Davis, *Harris Harding,* p. 101.
91 *Ibid.,* pp. 102-103.
92 Quoted in Cramp, "History", p. 94.
93 Quoted in *ibid.,* pp. 94-5.
94 See the figures in *ibid.,* p. 95.
95 *Ibid.* , p. 100.
96 *Ibid.*
97 Davis, *Harris Harding,* p. 149.

98   *Ibid.*, p. 136.

99   *Ibid.*, pp. 136-7.

100 See how this thesis regarding applying one "Awakening" paradigm to another "Awakening" is developed in R.D. Shiels, "The Connecticut Clergy in the Second Great Awakening" (Unpublished Ph.D. thesis, Boston University, 1976) and in his "The Myth of the Second Great Awakening".

Church Covenants and Church Discipline Among Baptists in the Maritime Provinces, 1778 - 1878

1   J. K. Zeman, *Baptist Roots and Identity* (Brantford: Baptist Convention of Ontario and Quebec, 1978), p. 4.

2   *Minutes*, New Brunswick Baptist Association, 1832, p. 14. (Hereafter, Baptist Association will be designated by BA.)

3   *Minutes*, Western Nova Scotia BA, 1863, p. 18.

4   *Minutes*, Eastern Nova Scotia BA, 1864, pp. 15-16.

5   Acadia University Archives (hereafter A.U.A.), Wolfville, N.S., J.M. Bumsted, "Origins of the Maritime Baptists: A New Document," typed MS., p. 5.

6   A.U.A., Minutes, Falmouth Baptist Church, January 23, 1870.

7   A.U.A., Minutes, Horton Baptist Church, Nov. 14 and 21, 1778.

8   *Ibid.*, February 1, 1862.

9   *Ibid.*, November 3, 1860.

10 *Ibid.*

11 *Ibid.*, January 4, 1862.

12 For the actual texts and a discussion of the origins and

historical development of the major covenants used in the period under consideration, see Charles W. Deweese, "Prominent Church Covenants of Maritime Baptists, 1778-1878," *Baptist History and Heritage,* Oct., 1980.

13 *Minutes,* Western New Brunswick BA, 1863, p. 14.

14 *Minutes,* Eastern Nova Scotia BA, 1871, pp. 16-17.

15 *Ibid.,* 1874, p. 13.

16 *Minutes,* New Brunswick BA, 1830, pp. 5-6.

17 *Minutes,* Nova Scotia BA, 1825, pp. 6-7; *Minutes,* New Brunswick BA, 1830, pp. 6-7; *Minutes,* Western New Brunswick BA, 1863, pp. 15-17.

18 *Minutes,* New Brunswick BA, 1830, p. 7; *Minutes,* Eastern Nova Scotia BA, 1858, pp. 11-12; *Minutes,* Eastern New Brunswick BA, 1880, p. 14.

19 *Minutes,* Nova Scotia BA, 1825, p. 6.

20 *Ibid.,* p. 8; *Ibid.,* 1838, pp. 16-17; *Minutes,* Eastern Nova Scotia BA, 1863, p. 11.

21 *Minutes,* Nova Scotia BA, 1838, p. 17.

22 *Ibid.,* p. 18.

23 *Ibid.,* 1825, p. 8.

24 *Ibid.,* 1838, p. 15.

25 *Minutes,* Western Nova Scotia BA, 1859, p. 14.

26 *Minutes,* Western New Brunswick BA, 1860, p. 13.

27 *Minutes,* Baptist Convention of Nova Scotia, New Brunswick, and Prince Edward Island, 1853, p. 21.

28 *Minutes,* Eastern New Brunswick BA, 1880, p. 13.

29 *Ibid.,* pp. 14-16.

30 *Minutes,* Central Nova Scotia BA, 1854, pp. 13-14.

31 *Minutes,* Eastern Nova Scotia BA, 1858, p. 10.

32 *Minutes,* Western New Brunswick BA, 1860, p. 13.

33 *Minutes,* Nova Scotia BA, 1838, p. 14.

34 A.U.A., Minutes, Nova Scotia Association (Congregational and Baptist), June 15, 1798.

35   *Ibid.*, June 16, 1798.

36   *Minutes*, African BA of Nova Scotia, 1867, p. 5.

37   *Ibid.*, 1871, p. 3.

38   *Minutes,* Nova Scotia and New Brunswick, BA, 1815, p. 5.

39   *Minutes*, Nova Scotia BA, 1836, p. 8.

40   *Minutes*, Nova Scotia and New Brunswick BA, 1814, p. 20.

41   *Minutes*, New Brunswick BA, 1822, p. 5.

42   A.U.A., "Church Articles," Nova Scotia and New Brunswick BA, 1808.

43   *Minutes*, New Brunswick BA, 1832, pp. 14-15.

44   Besides being repeated in the 1841 and 1845 minutes of the New Brunswick Association, they also appeared in the minutes of the Western New Brunswick Association (1848, 1850, 1852, 1855, 1857, 1859, 1862, 1864, 1867, 1869-76, 1878), the Eastern New Brunswick Association (1849, 1853, 1855, 1859, 1862-63, 1867, 1869-73, 1875-76, 1878), and the African Baptist Association of Nova Scotia (1869). Although these statements were apparently not printed in the minutes of the other Nova Scotia associations, they were included in the pamphlet *A Declaration of the Faith, Practice & Covenant of the Churches of Christ Composing the Nova Scotia Baptist Associations* (Halifax: Christian Messenger Office, 1855), pp. 5-7.

45   *Minutes*, Baptist Convention of Nova Scotia, New Brunswick, and Prince Edward Island, 1852, p. 17.

46   *A Treatise on the Faith of the Free Christian Baptists in Nova Scotia and New Brunswick* (St. John: Bailey & Day, 1848), p. 15.

47   *Minutes*, Free Christian Baptist General Conference of New Brunswick, 1857, pp. 28-32; 1864, pp. 37-40; Free Baptist Conference of Nova Scotia, 1866, pp. 10-13.

48   *Minutes*, Free Christian Baptist General Conference of

New Brunswick, 1855, p. 32; 1864, p. 33.

49 *Ibid.*
50 *Minutes*, Free Baptist Conference of Nova Scotia, 1866, p. 15; 1877, pp. 39-40.
51 *Minutes*, Free Christian Baptist General Conference of New Brunswick, 1868, pp. 36-37.
52 *Ibid.*, p. 37.
53 *Ibid.*
54 *Ibid.*
55 (St. John: George W. Day, 1873), pp. 23-26.
56 *Minutes*, Free Christian Baptist General Conference of New Brunswick, 1860, p. 11.
57 A.U.A., Minutes, Fredericton Baptist Church, December 9, 1815.
58 A.U.A., Minutes, North River Baptist Church, May 1, 1869.
59 A.U.A., Minutes, Baptist Church at Prince William and Queensbury, January 13, 1810.
60 A.U.A., Minutes, Onslow Baptist Church, December 22, 1867.
61 A.U.A., Minutes, Alexandra Baptist Church, January 10, 1844.
62 A.U.A., Minutes, Cornwallis Baptist Church, February 12, 1820.
63 A.U.A., Minutes, Alexandra Baptist Church, June, 1845.
64 A.U.A., Minutes, Horton Baptist Church, July 31, 1852.
65 *Ibid.*, April 6, 1799.
66 *Ibid.*, September 5, 1857.
67 *Ibid.*, January 4, 1862.
68 *Ibid.*
69 *Ibid.*, December 3, 1864.
70 *Ibid.*, July 9, 1870.

71 A.U.A., Minutes, Fredericton Baptist Church, January 23, 1878.

The Role of the African United Baptist Association In the Development of Indigenous Afro-Canadians in Nova Scotia, 1782-1978

1 *Canadian Census* (Ottawa: Statistics Canada, 1971-1976).

2 *Ibid.,* 1971, 1976.

3 T.B. Akins, "History of Halifax City", *Collections of the Nova Scotia Historical Society,* vol. VIII, 1899, p. 235.

4 Peter E. MacKerrow, *A Brief History of the Coloured Baptists of Nova Scotia, and Their First Organization as Churches, A.D. 1832* (Halifax, 1895); Pearleen Oliver, *A Brief History of the Coloured Baptists of Nova Scotia, 1782-1953* (Halifax, 1953).

5 Joseph R. Washington, Jr., *Black Religion: The Negro and Christianity in the United States* (Boston, 1964), p. 52.

6 Thomas Raddall, *Halifax, Warden of the North* (Toronto, 1948), pp. 20-30.

7 Quoted in T. Watson Smith, "The Slave in Canada", *Collections of the Nova Scotia Historical Society,* Vol. XX, p. 9.

8 Public Archives of Nova Scotia, Halifax, N.S., Owen Scrap Book, No. 2, *Slavery Days in Nova Scotia,* p. 111; "Coloured Slave Bought in Truro", *Truro Daily News,* June 8, 1926, p. 1.

9 George Patterson (ed.), *A Few Remains of the Rev. James MacGregor, D.D.* (Philadelphia, 1859), pp. 169-188.

10 William Renwick Riddell, "The Baptism of Slaves in Prince Edward Island," *Journal of Negro History,* Volume 6, July 7, 1921, pp. 307-309.

11 I.E. Bill, *Fifty Years with the Baptist Ministers and Churches of the Maritime Province of Canada* (St. John: Barnes and Company, 1880), p. 20.

12 *Ibid.,* p. 22.

13 *Ibid.,* p. 23.

14 *Ibid.,* p. 23.

15 *Ibid.,* p. 22.

16 C.B. Fergusson (ed.), *Clarkson's Mission to America, 1791-1792.* (Halifax: Public Archives of Nova Scotia, 1971), pp. 13-14.

17 *Ibid.,* pp. 149,161.

18 Bill, *op. cit.,* p. 32.

19 *Ibid.,* p. 32.

20 *Ibid.,* p. 32.

21 *Ibid.,* p. 32.

22 *Ibid.,* p. 32.

23 *Ibid.,* p. 32.

24 *Ibid.,* pp. 32-33.

25 "The Baptists of Nova Scotia, From A.D. 1828 to A.D. 1838," in *Christian Messenger* (Halifax; Wednesday, Januray 29, 1862), p. 33.

26 *Ibid.,* p. 33.

27 *Minutes of the Eighth Session of the African Baptist Association of Nova Scotia* (Halifax, 1861), p. 6.

28 *Ibid.,* p. 6.

29 MacKerrow, *op.cit.,* p. 18.

30 *Ibid.,* p. 18.

31 *Ibid.,* p. 19.

32 *Ibid.,* p. 19.

33 *Ibid.,* p. 20.

34 Washington, *op.cit.,* Chapters 1, 3, and 4; James H. Cone, *A Black Theology of Liberation* (New York: J.B. Lippincott Company, 1970).

35 MacKerrow, *op.cit.,* p. 15.

36 *Minutes of the Session of the African Baptist Association* (Halifax, 1854), p. 2.

37 *Ibid.*

38 Washington, *op. cit.*, p. 52.

39 *Minutes of the Session of the African Baptist Association.* 1854, p. 3.

40 *The Novascotian,* 1846, p. 6.

41 *Ibid.*, p. 6.

42 *Minutes of the Session of the African Baptist Association,* 1861, p. 2.

43 MacKerrow, *op. cit.*, p. 31.

44 *Ibid.*, p. 32.

45 *Minutes of the Fourteenth Session of the African Baptist Association* (Halifax, 1867), p. 5.

46 *Ibid.*, p. 5.

47 MacKerrow, *op. cit.*, p. 33.

48 *Minutes of the Sixteenth Session of the African Baptist Association* (Halifax, 1869), p. 10.

49 *Ibid.*, p. 10.

50 *Minutes of the Nineteenth Session of the African Baptist Association* (Halifax, 1872), p. 13.

51 *Minutes of the Sixteenth Session,* pp. 1-7.

52 *Minutes of the Thirtieth Annual Session of the African Baptist Association* (Halifax, 1884), p. 8.

53 *Minutes of the Twenty-fourth Session of the African Baptist Association* (Halifax, 1877), p. 8.

54 *Minutes of the Fifty-First Annual Session of the African Baptist Association* (Halifax, 1904), p. 9.

55 Office of the Dean of Law, Dalhousie University, Halifax, N.S., list of the members of the graduating class of 1898.

56 *Minutes of the African Baptist Association* (Halifax, 1930 and 1935).

57 *Minutes of the Forty-Seventh Annual Session of the African Baptist Association of Nova Scotia* (Halifax, 1900), p. 5.

58 *Minutes of the Fiftieth Annual Session of the African*

Baptist Assocation (Halifax, 1903), p. 17.

59 *Minutes of the Twenty-Seventh Annual Session of the African Baptist Association* (Halifax, 1880), p. 10.

60 *Minutes of the 68th Meeting of the African United Baptist Association of Nova Scotia* (Halifax, 1921), p. 39.

61 *Ibid.*, p. 39.

62 *Ibid.*, p. 36.

63 *Ibid.*, p. 36.

64 *Ibid.*, p. 39.

65 *Ibid.*, p. 39.

66 *Minutes of the 64th Meeting of the African United Baptist Association of Nova Scotia* (Halifax, 1917), pp. 29-30.

67 Acadia University Archives, Wolfville, N.S., Constitution, Ladies Auxiliary of the African Baptist Association, "Objects".

68 *Minutes of the Thirtieth Session,* p. 16.

69 *Minutes of the 67th Meeting of the African United Baptist Association of Nova Scotia* (Halifax, 1920), p. 21.

70 *Minutes of the 66th Meeting of the African United Baptist Association of Nova Scotia* (Halifax, 1919), p. 23.

71 *Minutes of the Sixty-Third Annual Session of the African Baptist Association of Nova Scotia.* (Halifax 1916), pp. 4-5.

72 *Ibid.*, p. 4.

73 *Minutes of the 77th Annual Session of the African Baptist Association of Nova Scotia* (Halifax, 1930), p. 5.

74 *83rd Meeting of the African United Baptist Association of Nova Scotia* (Halifax, 1936), p. 46.

75 *Minutes of the 98th Annual Meeting of the African United Baptist Association of Nova Scotia* (Halifax, 1951), p. 33.

76 *Minutes of the African United Baptist Associaton of Nova Scotia, 111th Session* (Halifax, 1964), p. 16.

77 *Minutes of the 121st Session of the African United Baptist*

Association of Nova Scotia (Halifax, 1974), p. 59.

78 *118th Session of the African United Baptist Association of Nova Scotia* (Halifax, 1971), p. 52.

"Joseph Howe is Their Devil": Controversies among Regular Baptists in Halifax, 1827-1868

1 William H. Munroe, "Religious Denominations,"*Lates: Illustrated Family Reference Bible* (Cincinnati: Forshee & McMakin, 1876), p. 2.

2 E. M.Saunders, *History of the Baptists of the Maritime Provinces* (Halifax: Press of John Burgoyne, 1902), pp. 394-435.

3 This church is not to be confused with the present First Baptist Church, Halifax. The present First Baptist Church appears in the paper as Granville Street Baptist Church.

4 Stephen Davidson, "Leaders of the Black Baptists of Nova Scotia, 1782-1832" (B. A. Honours Thesis, Acadia University, 1975), pp. 27-38.

5 *Minutes of the Nova Scotia Baptist Association* (Halifax: J. H. White, 1827).

6 George E. Levy, *The Baptists of the Maritime Provinces* (Saint John: Barnes-Hopkins, Ltd., 1946), pp. 110-112.

7 The theme is inspired by current ecumenical dialogue. See John Macquarrie, *Christian Unity and Christian Diversity* (London: SCM Press Ltd., 1975).

8 Philip G. A. Allwood, "First Baptist Church, Halifax: Its Origin and Early Years" (M. Div. Thesis, Acadia University, 1978), pp. 39-44.

9 George W. Hill, "History of St. Paul's Church No. IV," *Collections of the Nova Scotia Historical Society for the years 1878-1884* (Belleville, Ontario: Mika Publishing Company), Vol. III, pp. 13-70.

10   Anonymous, *Origin and Formation of the Baptist Church in Granville Street, Halifax, Nova Scotia* (Boston: Lincoln & Edmands, 1828), p. 20.

11   Acadia University Archives, Wolfville, N.S. (hereafter A.U.A.), Manning Correspondence, vol. IV, John Burton to Edward Manning, May, 1825.

12   A.U.A., Scrapbook, J.M. Cramp, "The Baptists of Nova Scotia (1760-1860)." These articles appeared in the *Christian Messenger,* Jan. 18, 1860-Sept. 23, 1863.

13   A.U.A., Manning Correspondence, vol. V, John Burton to Council, Feb., 1828.

14   A.U.A., Manning Correspondence, vol. V, Alexander Crawford to Richard Creed, January 13, 1828.

15   Anonymous, *Origin . . .,* pp. 24-33.

16   *Proceedings of the Nova Scotia Baptist Education Society 1828-1832* (Halifax: *Nova Scotian,* 1832), pp. 31-32.

17   I.E. Bill, *Fifty Years with the Baptist Ministers and Churches of the Maritime Provinces* (Saint John: Barnes and Company, 1880), pp. 314-315.

18   Cramp, *op.cit.,* p. 259.

19   A.U.A., Manning Correspondence, vol. III, John Ferguson to Edward Manning, Aug. 24, 1824.

20   A.U.A., Manning Correspondence, vol. V, John Ferguson to Edward Manning, January 3, 1827.

21   E.A. Crawley, "The Rise and Progress of Higher Education in Connection with the Baptist Denomination in the Maritime Provinces," in *Memorials of Acadia College and Horton Academy* (Montreal: Dawson Brothers, Publishers, 1881), p. 27; A.U.A., Manning Correspondence, vol. V, John Ferguson to Edward Manning, January 12, 1827.

22   A.U.A., Manning Correspondence, vol. V, John Burton to Council, Feb., 1828.

23   *Ibid.*

24 *Ibid.*

25 Public Archives of Nova Scotia, Halifax, N.S., Vertical Manuscript File, "Halifax Churches, Historical Facts about the First Baptist," *Evening Mail,* May 21, 1881.

26 A.U.A., Manning Correspondence, vol. V, John Burton to Council, Feb., 1828.

27 A.U.A., Manning Correspondence, vol. VI, Report of the Council called due to the Problems in Burton's Church, January 29-February 4, 1828.

28 *Minutes of the Nova Scotia Baptist Association* (Halifax: *The Acadian,* 1829).

29 R.M. Hattie, "Old Time Halifax Churches," *Collections of the Nova Scotia Historical Society,* XXVI, 1945 (Halifax: 1946), p. 4.

30 *Minutes of the Nova Scotia Baptist Association* (Halifax: *Christian Messenger* Office, 1841).

31 A.U.A., Manning Correspondence, vol. V, John Ferguson to Edward Manning, November 27, 1827.

32 *Minutes of the Nova Scotia Baptist Association* (Halifax: Philip J. Holland, 1832).

33 See Peter E. McKerrow, *A brief History of the Coloured Baptists of Nova Scotia (1832-1895)* (Halifax: Nova Scotia Printing Co., 1895).

34 Public Archives of Nova Scotia, Manuscript Group 4 41, Granville Street Baptist Church Record Book 1827-1842, pp. 12-27.

35 Robert T. Handy, *A History of the Churches in the United States and Canada* (Oxford: Clarendon Press, 1976), p. 169.

36 Munroe, *loc.cit.*

37 Levy, *op.cit.,* pp. 97-98.

38 P.H. Ballard, "Baptists in Scotland Before 1869," *The Baptist Quarterly,* XXIII (April 1970), pp. 256-257.

39 Compare Hattie, *op.cit.,* pp. 2-5, and Granville Street Baptist Church Record Book 1827-1842, *op.cit.*

40 Ballard, *op.cit.*, p. 256.

41 R.E. Shaw, "History of the Disciples of Christ in Halifax, N.S.," *Collections of the Nova Scotia Historical Society,* XXXIV (1963), p. 123.

42 Allwood, *op.cit.*, pp. 71-72. Pryor went to Newton Theological Institute and Crawley went to Andover Seminary.

43 *Ibid.*, pp. 73-79.

44 *Ibid.*, pp. 79-83.

45 *Ibid.*, pp. 92-94.

46 Granville Street Baptist Church Record Book, *op.cit.*, pp. 65-68.

47 Shaw, *op.cit.*, p. 125.

48 Granville Street Baptist Church Record Book, *op.cit.*, p. 100.

49 See Shaw, *op.cit.*

50 *Minutes of the Nova Scotia Baptist Association* (Halifax: James Spike, 1834), p. 8.

51 A.U.A., Manning Correspondence, vol. VIII, I. E. Bill to Edward Manning, January 29, 1835.

52 Hattie, *op.cit.*, pp. 48-61.

53 E.M. Saunders, *A Sketch of the Origin and History of the Granville Street Baptist Church* (Halifax: *Christian Messenger* Office, 1877), p. 28.

54 Joseph Belcher, "A Letter to the Members of the Baptist Church and Congregation assembling in Granville Street" (Halifax: 1845), p. 20.

55 *Ibid.*, p. 24.

56 Philip G. A. Allwood, "The Belcher Schism," (Essay #4 CH 782, Acadia Divinity College, 1978), p. 16.

57 A.U.A., John Pryor to J.W. Nutting, November 16, 1844.

58 I. E. Bill, *op. cit.*, pp. 114-115.

59 Albert Coldwell, "History of Acadia College," *Memorials*

of Acadia College and Horton Academy, op. cit., pp. 70-73.

60 In 1834, Nutting and Ferguson became the editors of the *Baptist Missionary Magazine,* which had been started in 1827 under the Reverend Charles Tupper's editorship. It was replaced with the *Chrisitan Messenger* in 1837 under the management of the same editors. Levy, *op. cit.,* p. 143.

61 *Ibid.,* p. 144.

62 Public Archives of New Brunswick, Fredericton, N.B. Coy Correspondence, MBL 5/10, Asa Coy to Mary Ann Coy, July 13, 1845.

63 A.U.A., John Pryor to J. W. Nutting, November 16, 1844.

64 Belcher, *op. cit.,* pp. 14-20.

65 "Letter from the Granville Street Church, December 24, 1845" (Halifax: 1846).

66 Joseph Belcher, "A Letter to James W. Nutting, Esquire" (Halifax: English and Blackadar, 1846), p. 9.

67 Anonymous, "Sketch of the History (to 1897) of the Baptists in the City and County of Halifax," (1897?), pp. 7-8.

68 Levy, *op.cit.,* p. 176.

69 Saunders, *loc.cit.*

70 *Ibid.,* pp. 27-28.

71 B.H. Eaton, *Reply to the Letter Addressed to Them by the Hon. J.W. Johnston* (Halifax: Barnes' Steam Press, 1868), pp. 6-41.

72 The Nova Scotia Baptist Association had divided itself into three Associations in 1850. Bill, *op.cit.,* p. 107.

73 *Minutes of the 17th Session of the Central Baptist Association of Nova Scotia* (Halifax: *Christian Messenger* Office, 1867), p. 6.

74 Eaton, *op.cit.,* pp. 46-78.

75 A.U.A., Church Records, "List of the officers and members of the Granville Street Baptists, 1883."

76 Payzant was a Halifax lawyer. He, J.W. Johnston, and J.W. Johnston, Jr. had left the Granville Street Baptist Church. They were received into the Dartmouth Baptist Church without a dismission from the Granville Street Church. This caused a controversy but was accepted because of the difficulties in the Halifax situation. *Christian Messenger,* June 24, 1868, p. 210, col. 2-4.

77 John Young Payzant, *Church Government: A Letter to Rev. E. M. Saunders* (Halifax: *Halifax Citizen* Steam Press, 1868).

78 *Minutes of the 18th Session of the Central Baptist Association of Nova Scotia* (Halifax: *Christian Messenger* Office, 1868), pp. 7-9. For details on the controversy see Philip G.A. Allwood, "The Excommunication of John Pryor" (Essay # 1 C H 642, Acadia Divinity College, 1976).

The Maritime Baptists and Higher Education in the Early Nineteenth Century

1 Gordon Stewart and George Rawlyk, '*A People Highly Favoured of God': The Nova Scotia Yankees and The American Revolution* (Toronto: Macmillan of Canada, 1972), p. 84.

2 John Davis, *Life and Times of the Late Rev. Harris Harding, Yarmouth, N.S.* (Charlottetown, 1866),p. 178.

3 Jack Bumsted, *Henry Alline* (Toronto, 1971), p. 62.

4 quoted in *ibid.* , p. 63.

5 Acadia University Archives (hereafter A.U.A.), Wolfville, N.S., Diary of Edward Manning, October 18, 1814.

6 Barry Moody, unpublished article on Charles Tupper, to

be included in *Dictionary of Canadian Biography,* vol. XI.

7 quoted in Davis, *op.cit.,* p. 126, Harding to editors of the *Christian Messenger,* July 14, 1846.

8 A.U.A., Diary of Edward Manning, June 3, 1814.

9 *Ibid.,* Dec. 6, 1818.

10 *Ibid.,* Aug. 10, 1821.

11 *Ibid.,* Aug. 2, 1821.

12 *Ibid.,* Aug. 6, 1821.

13 A.U.A., Manning Correspondence, vol.5, Edward Harris to Edward Manning, April 23, 1827.

14 *Baptist Missionary Magazine for Nova Scotia and New Brunswick,* July, 1831, pp. 109-112, letter from R to the editors.

15 *Christian Messenger,* July 27, 1838, p. 239, letter from A.O.B. to the editors.

16 *Ibid.,* Dec. 14, 1838, p. 399, "Journal of a Lay Preacher."

17 quoted in Davis, pp. 134-5.

18 A.U.A., Manning Correspondence, vol. 5, Manning to Richard McClearn, July 4, 1828.

19 *Christian Messenger,* April 7, 1837, pp. 110-111, "Why Should Ministers Attend a Place of Education?" by a Correspondent.

20 *Ibid.,* March 3, 1837, pp. 68-9, J.D. to the editors.

21 *Ibid.,* April 28, 1837, p. 135, "Why Should Ministers Attend a Place of Education?" #2, by A Correspondent.

22 *Baptist Missionary Magazine,* July, 1831, pp. 109-112, R to the editors.

23 A.U.A., Manning Correspondence, vol. 6, Henry Blakner to Edward Manning, April 24, 1829.

24 A.U.A., Diary of Edward Manning, Nov. 29, 1818.

25 *Christian Messenger,* June 8, 1838, p. 179.

26 A.U.A., Diary of Edward Manning, May 17, 1819.

27 *Ibid.*, Aug. 23, 1820.

28 *Ibid.*, Nov. 4, 1817.

29 *The Report of the Nova Scotia Baptist Education Committee* (Halifax, 1835), p. 3.

30 A.U.A., Manning Correspondence, vol. 5, Samuel Elder to Edward Manning, Jan. 17, 1826.

31 *Christian Messenger,* June 16, 1837, p. 190, an open letter to the Baptist Association at Yarmouth from a True Friend of the Horton Academy.

32 *Report of the Nova Scotia Baptist Education Society* (Halifax, 1836), p. 7.

33 *Christian Messenger,* Oct. 19, 1838, pp. 332-3, E. A. Crawley to the editor of the *Novascotian,* Letter #4.

34 *Ibid.,* Nov. 30, 1838, pp. 377-8, Address...to the Members of the Baptist Churches and Congregations, and other persons friendly to Education, in the Provinces of Nova Scotia, New Brunswick, and Prince Edward Island.

35 See A.U.A., Diary of Edward Manning, 1826-1828.

36 *Ibid.*, Sept. 12, 1827, Sept. 13, 1827.

37 *Report of the Nova Scotia Baptist Education Society* (Halifax, 1832), p. 26.

38 *Report of the Nova Scotia Baptist Education Society,* 1835, p. 3.

39 *Christian Messenger,* June 16, 1837, p. 190, letter to the Baptist Association at Yarmouth from a True Friend of Horton Academy.

40 *Christian Messenger,* Feb. 23, 1838, pp. 58-9.

41 *Ibid.*, Nov. 30, 1838, pp. 377-8.

42 *Report of the Nova Scotia Baptist Education Society* (Halifax, 1832), pp. 21-2.

43 *Christian Messenger,* Mar. 23, 1838, pp. 90-1.

The New Brunswick Baptist Seminary
1833-1895

See W.S. MacNutt, *New Brunswick A History: 1784-1867* (Toronto, 1963). On the emergence of the temperance movement in this period and related social issues see W.H. Elgee, *The Social Teachings of the Canadian Churches Protestant 1750-1850* (Toronto, 1959), *passim*.

Walter R. Greenwood, *The Early Baptists of Cambridge Parish* (Jemseg, N.B., 1941), pp. 6ff., mentions the ministerial labours of Edward Manning, Joseph Crandall, Elijah Estabrooks, Charles Lewis and W.H. Beckwith.

3 *Minutes of the New Brunswick Baptist Association* (hereafter referred to as N.B.B.A.), Norton, 1830, p. 8. Cf. *Corresponding Letter N.B.B.A.,* Waterbury, 1829, p. 12: "With many of our churches, the state of religion is low, and the cause of God in a languishing condition. They are hanging their harps upon the willows: yet we trust exertions will be used to endeavour, under the blessing of God, to invigorate these little hills of Zion scattered up and down this wilderness country." The report noted "a manifest want of vigorous and systematic exertion on the part of the Churches in assisting towards a constant or periodical supply of ministerial labour." It added: "But we trust the day is not far distant when the Churches will be aroused to a sense of duty in this respect."

4 *Ibid.* They were concerned "for the extensive spread of the gospel of the blessed God, and the advancement of the Kingdom of the Messiah."

5 These words were actually used by Captain George W. Masters in laying the cornerstone of St. Martins Seminary (see *The Daily Sun*, Saint John, July 21, 1886), but they reflect the attitude of the founders from the beginning.

6 On the contribution of Maritime Baptists to higher education see W.E. O'Grady, "The Fathers and Higher Education" (B.D. thesis, Acadia University, 1953). O'Grady concentrates on Nova Scotia, and largely overlooks the development of the New Brunswick Baptist Seminary. However, he notes the interest in education of Joseph Crandall who for many years served as President of the New Brunswick Baptist Education Society.

7 It must be remembered that it was not until 1871 that the Common School Act established grammar and superior schools throughout New Brunswick. There was thus a need for general education in the days before the establishment of the provincial system.

8 Acadia University Archives (hereafter A.U.A.), Wolfville, N.S., Records of the New Brunswick Baptist Education Society (hereafter N.B.B.E.S.), John T. Smith, Secretary of the Committee of Management, to Rev. C. Bosworth, October 13, 1842. Cf. N.B.B.E.S. Annual Report for 1866 (in the *Minutes of the Western New Brunswick Baptist Association,* hereafter referred to as W.N.B.B.A., Newcastle, 1866, p. 37): "One of the objects of the Society, from its formation, has been to impart suitable instruction to young men who desire to preach the Gospel, and may not be able to avail themselves of a full collegiate course." While several attempts were made at theological education under Dr. Spurden, these proved abortive. One such attempt is recorded in the minutes for June 6, 1867 (N.B.B.E.S. Records, 1834-72): "Resolved, That the Provincial grant of $1,000 and the tuition fees, be given to Professor Hopper to carry on the Literary Department of the Institution, and that the Theological Department be placed under the control of Rev. Dr. C. Spurden, his salary to be paid by the Denomination." It was then moved "that Rev. J.C. Hurd [then pastor of the Fredericton Baptist Church] be appointed to visit the Churches with special reference to raising the salary for Dr. Spurden, and to excite a more general interest in favour of secular and ministerial education." While the

operations of the Society during its first few years were largely confined to "general education", the Committee of Management regarded "the establishment of a theological department" as a matter of "vital importance". See the *Baptist Magazine* (London, 1841), pp. 21, 22.

9   I.E. Bill, *Fifty Years with the Baptist Ministers and Churches of the Maritime Provinces* (Saint John, 1880), p. 582.

10   Philip Allwood, "Elevating the Standard: The Fredericton Seminary," *The Atlantic Baptist,* February 1, 1979, p. 15 (35). In the late 1830's New Brunswick Baptists were being asked to support collegiate educational work in Nova Scotia on a temporary basis "until the time shall come when they feel themselves ripe for a College in New Brunswick." This proviso was conveniently forgotten by men like H.C. Creed when they desired to concentrate all the Baptist educational work in Wolfville. See Herbert C. Creed, *A Baptist Academy for New Brunswick* (Fredericton: Daily and Weekly Herald Office, 1882). Two of the principal advocates of the original Seminary were the Rev. F.W. Miles and W.B. Kinnear, whose careers have been briefly described by G.E. Levy, "The New Brunswick Baptist Seminary," *The Atlantic Baptist,* May 15, 1975, p. 3 (115). E.M. Saunders, *The History of the Baptists of the Maritime Provinces* (Halifax, 1902), p. 489, has a brief biographical note on Kinnear, noting his contributions to the legal profession, politics, the Bible Society and the Y.M.C.A. Kinnear was elected to the New Brunswick Assembly in September 1830, appointed to the Legislative Council in February 1839, and served as Solicitor-General from 1846 to 1854. On F.W. Miles, T.D. Denham, (ed.), *The History of Germain St. Baptist Church, Saint John, N.B. (1810-1910)* (Saint John, 1910), pp. 23, 24, provides a few details not mentioned by Levy, noting that Miles was ordained in 1828 and became the seventh pastor of Germain St.: "During his pastorate of three years, fifty were received by baptism. In the autumn of 1830, Mr. Miles resigned for the purpose of completing

his theological course at Newton." F.W. Miles was the son of a Colonel T. Odbur Miles of Long Island, New York, who had settled in Maugerville, N.B., after receiving a large land grant from the British government in return for services rendered during the American Revolution.

11   The members of this committee were the Rev. F.W. Miles, W.B. Kinnear, John H. Wilmot, the Rev. Joseph Crandall, the Rev. John Marsters, the Rev. Samuel Robinson and William Needham. Allwood, *op. cit.*, following Bill, *op. cit.*, p. 323 , and *The Seminary Bema,* April, 1893, p. 63, mistakenly attributes a major role in the preparation of the prospectus to Jarvis Ring, who is not even mentioned in the association minutes as a member of the committee appointed to draw up the prospectus *(Minutes of the N.B.B.A.,* St. George, 1833, p. 6)! According to the recently rediscovered "Memoirs of Jarvis Ring," in the possession of George and Carl Allwood of Halifax, N.S. and St. John, N.B., all Jarvis Ring claimed to do with "Brother Miles and some other leading members" was to "agitate the question" at the association and to "draw up a rough draft of what sort of a building was wanted and in what part of the province it should be located" (p. 76). It is true that Ring alludes to a different committee appointed at the St. George Association consisting of George Miles, John T. Smith, Aaron Hartt and himself. Perhaps these were the "leading members" who with Miles drew up the initial rough draft for presentation to the association. This supposition might explain why there is no mention of this committee in the association minutes. Its work was only exploratory and preliminary, and after the association had considered the case for the establishment of a Seminary, detailed plans were laid and proper committees appointed. Useful biographical information on Jarvis Ring, who was one of the founders of both the Fredericton (now Brunswick St.) Baptist Church and the New Brunswick Baptist Seminary is provided in obituaries by W.L. Hopkins, *Minutes of the W.N.B.B.A.,* St. George, 1868, p. 11, and Charles Tupper, *Baptist Year Book,* 1868, p. 31. Cf. also Bill, *op. cit.,* pp.

321-27.

12 Membership statistics, *Minutes of the N.B.B.A.,* 1833, p. 3.

13 *The New Brunswick Courier,* September 21, 1833, reporting on the first meeting of the N.B.B.E.S., resolved "that as soon as a sufficient sum shall be subscribed, the Committee of Management be authorized to proceed with the erection of a suitable building...." It was also decided that the Annual Meeting of the Society would be held "at the time and place at which the New Brunswick Baptist Association meets."

14 A.U.A., N.B.B.E.S. Records, 1834-1872; the Constitution is reprinted in *The New Brunswick Courier,* September 21, 1833, p. 12 and *The Christian Visitor,* January 18, 1866, p. 2.

15 *Minutes of the N.B.B.A.,* Saint John, 1834, p. 8. In the Digest of the Letters from the Churches of 1834 it was reported that F.W. Miles had settled as pastor in Fredericton, "a Pastor whom they regard with great affection" (p. 8). The note added: "They [the Fredericton Baptist Church] are cordially engaged in the support of the Baptist Education Society, which has determined to erect the Seminary there." According to advertisements in *The New Brunswick Courier* (e.g., April 19, 1834, p. 1), Miles in 1834 was also serving as the agent of the *Baptist Missionary Magazine of Nova Scotia and New Brunswick.* The Fredericton location for the Seminary was described in the denominational records as "a most pleasant and eligible site" (*Minutes of the N.B.B.A.,* Prince William, 1835, p. 7). A detailed advertisement for the new Seminary appeared in *The New Brunswick Courier,* December 5, 1835, p. 2.

16 According to Jarvis Ring, *op. cit.,* p. 76, three quarters of an acre of land was originally purchased (330 ft. x 99 ft.) from a Mr. Street. The Fredericton Baptist Church bought the Brunswick St. corner (110 ft. x 99 ft.). That left the new Seminary with a lot on the corner of Carleton (now York) and George Streets with dimensions of 220 ft.

x 99 ft.

17 Jarvis Ring, *op. cit.,* p. 76, states plainly: "The building was commenced in 1833 and finished in 1835." By this statement, however, he may only mean that the plans for the building were launched in 1833 and the actual construction was completed in 1835. That this is the more probable interpretation is suggested by the association minutes for 1834, where it was resolved that "the Committee of Management, having reported that the ground at Maugerville was not suitable for the erection of the Seminary, the Committee be instructed to erect the same at Fredericton." *(Minutes of the N.B.B.A.,* St. John, 1834, pp. 7-8). The same association resolved "that the Baptist Ministers of the Province be requested to take up Subscriptions in support of the said Seminary" *(ibid.,* p. 8), and the records of the Society show that this was done from June, 1834, onwards (A.U.A., N.B.B.E.S., Records, 1834-1872). Since the N.B.B.E.S. was only formally organized in September of 1833, it was quite impossible to commence the erection of the building in that year. The selection of the site, which Ring *(op. cit.,* p. 76) notes occasioned both division and delay, was not the only factor. The publicizing of the venture, canvassing for subscriptions and the calling for tenders all took time. The 1834 date for the actual commencement of construction allows time for all these necessary preparations, and is independently verified in *The New Brunswick Courier* (July 25, 1835, p. 2), which gives the Annual Report of the N.B.B.E.S. Delbert Bannister, "A Brief History of the Union Baptist Seminary," (A.U.A. typescript, 1971.). p. 2, it seems, is simply following uncritically a report in *The Seminary Bema,* April 1893, p. 64, which gives the date as 1833. Bill, *op. cit.,* p. 323, who also gives the date as 1833, is merely quoting Jarvis Ring, whose words we have seen are capable of another interpretation. G.E. Levy, *The Baptists of the Maritime Provinces* (Saint John, 1946), p. 121, correctly dates the commencement of work on the Seminary building. So

also *Minutes of the N.B.B.A.,* Saint John, 1834, p.8, and a Souvenir Directory of the Baptist Church, Fredericton, N.B., 1903, p. 5.

18 So Bannister, *op. cit.,* p.1, who cities *The Seminary Bema,* April 1893, p. 63. It is independently verified by Jarvis Ring, *op. cit.,* p. 76, who gives the figure as £2376.0.7½. A somewhat smaller amount is suggested in association minutes (£2120.15.8), but this probably does not include interest charges *(Minutes of the N.B.B.A.,* Salisbury, fortunately supplemented by a statement in 1837 *(Minutes of the N.B.B.A.,* Fredericton, p. 9): "The total cost of land, erection of buildings, fences, etc. is £2,376.05.7½d."

19 *Minutes of the N.B.B.A.,* Fredericton, 1837, p. 10, mentions a meeting of the Committee of Management of the Seminary held at the home of Jarvis Ring on June 4, 1837, where the petition of Burpee and Taylor was considered and turned down for four reasons stated by the Secretary, John T. Smith. Briefly, the Committee held that "the contractors have been amply rewarded for all alterations and extra work done...."

20 For subjects offered and tuition fees see the Seminary's advertisement in *The New Brunswick Courier,* December 5, 1835, p. 2. For an early report on the Seminary's work see *The New Brunswick Courier,* July 30, 1836, p. 2.

21 Levy, *The Baptists of the Maritime Provinces,* p. 121. cf. Saunders, *op.cit.,* p. 234. At both Saint John and St. Martins the Seminary was operated on co-educational lines. In 1890 Dr. Hopper carefully defined the term co-education: "By co-education we mean not simply that young men and women recite together in the same class rooms, but that they have a portion of their social life in common; that they sit at the same table for meals, and have so far as agreeable their recreations together; that they have equal rights and privileges in the course of study, in the literary societies and in the devotional and missionary meetings, etc." *(Messenger and Visitor,* December 17, 1890, Supplement,). In urging the values of

co-education Principal Hopper said: "The school is ordered after the model of a Christian home rather than a nunnery or cloister. We believe we are demonstrating the problem of co-education, and that the result is most gratifying and reassuring. The commingling of students of both sexes in the class room, the parlor, the dining hall, and the campus tends to the improvement of gentlemanly and ladylike conduct." *(Messenger and Visitor,* January 1, 1890, p. 1).

22 Philip G.A. Allwood, "First Baptist Church, Halifax: Its Origin and Early Years," (M.Div. thesis, Acadia Divinity College, 1978), p. 116, footnote 6 notes: "King's [College, Windsor, N.S.] had removed its requirement for graduation of signing the Thirty-Nine Articles in the 1827-1830 period", according to H.Y. Hind, *The University of King's College 1790-1890* (New York, 1890), p. 70. Fred H. Phillips in an article in the Fredericton paper *The Daily Gleaner,* April 20, 1965, incorrectly states that the Fredericton Seminary was "apparently" open to "students of other dissenting bodies". The correct adverb is "certainly", for the school prided itself in the non-sectarian character of its instruction and insisted from the first that its doors should be open to students from *all* denominations. Article 11 in the Constitution of the N.B.B.E.S. spelled out this principle very clearly, stating "that the Seminary will be open to persons of any religious denomination." See *The Christian Visitor,* January 18, 1866, p. 2, and *The New Brunswick Courier,* September 21, 1833, p. 12.

23 *Minutes of the N.B.B.A.,* Salisbury, 1836, p. 8. The same report acknowledged that this studious concern to achieve "entire freedom from all sectarian influence" was deliberate, for thereby "confidence has been given to persons of various religious sentiments, to seek here an education for their children." Note the remark of E.R. Fitch, (ed.), *The Baptists of Canada* (Toronto, 1911), p. 80: "At this time King's College, at Fredericton, a school exclusively for Episcopalians, was receiving $8,800

annually from provincial revenues. It also sustained a theological chair exclusively for the benefit of the Church of England." Fitch's statement reflects the resentment felt by many non-Anglicans at the privileged position given to Episcopalians, but he somewhat overstates the case when he asserts that the institution was "exclusively" for that one denomination. However, Anglican services were held in the chapel and the Principal of King's College was an ordained Anglican priest, so that the prevailing ethos of the college was sufficiently Anglican to make dissenters feel uncomfortable about sending their children to such an institution.

24 E.g., *Minutes of the N.B.B.A.,* Springfield, 1838, p. 24, recognized the need of "increased and united effort" to sustain the Seminary, and furnish its Committee of Management "with sufficient funds to relieve the Institution from its present pecuniary embarrassments." That same Annual Report resolved that "an efficient Agent be employed by the Committee to travel through the whole Province to make known the claims of the Institution to public support, and to invite all friends of education to assist in sustaining an object of so much public utility." An urgent appeal was also made to Britain, for it is mentioned in the first report of the Baptist Canadian Missionary Society held in Park St. Chapel, Southwark, December 5, 1838. See *Baptist Magazine* (London), 1839, p. 94. The report noted that the Seminary's "most ardent friends despair of its continued existence, unless prompt and generous assistance can be obtained. A debt of £200 threatens to crush the institution." Similarly when the petition for a government grant was turned down again in 1839 the Circular Letter raised the searching question: "Shall a denomination of nearly 3000 communicants, with probably five times that number connected with us as members of our congregations, and possessing the sentiments of the denomination, allow the operations of a useful institution to be suppressed by such opposition when we have the means of sustaining it within our power?" *(Minutes of the*

N.B.B.A., Canning, Queens Co., 1839). The Annual Report of the N.B.B.E.S. that year mentioned the "very great personal exertion and sacrifice" of the Committee of Management to sustain the Seminary financially. *(Minutes of the N.B.B.A.,* Canning, 1839, p. 22). The Circular Letter of 1848 similarly bemoaned the "absence of a spirit of Christian liberality." Several suffering causes were singled out, including the Seminary. Without "pecuniary aid", their pious protestations were "no better than a solemn mockery." *(Minutes of the N.B.B.A.,* Brussels, St., Saint John, 1848, pp. 12-13). In 1848 the debt was reduced to £92, largely by assistance from the Union Society. However, the Committee of Management just four years later was deterred "from attempting to liquidate the debt by the pressing claims of Acadia College". It was felt at that time that Acadia's "efficiency, if not its very existence" was at stake *(Minutes of the W.N.B.B.A.,* Prince William, 1852, p. 23). In 1853 Charles Spurden observed that in his ten years as Principal the amount paid out in debt charges was £345. *(Minutes of the W.N.B.B.A.,* St. George, 1853, p. 22).

25 After five unsuccessful annual appeals a legislative grant of £500 ($2000) was actually paid in 1840, and an annual grant of £250 was given in 1845. It is estimated that the total legislative grants up to 1869 amounted to $28,000. See *The Seminary Bema,* April 1893, p. 65. When the first request for a grant was turned down in 1835 by the Legislative Council, Jarvis Ring was quick to point out that it had been recommended by "about six hundred respectable individuals belonging to the several religious denominations in this Province, and passed by the almost unanimous vote of the House [of Assembly]." He also noted that "liberal grants have been made by the Legislature of a Sister colony [Nova Scotia] in aid of a similar institution [Acadia]." See *Minutes of the N.B.B.A.,* Prince William, 1835, p. 8. Similarly in the Annual Report of the Education Society delivered on July 10, 1838 at Springfield, Kings Co., blunt criticism was levelled against the Legislative Council for its prejudice in

blocking the annual application for a government grant "merely because the institution was principally established by the liberality and exertions of one denomination" *(Minutes of the N.B.B.A.,* Springfield, 1838, p. 23). The Report added: "...the conclusion is unavoidable that the claims of the Baptist Seminary have not been equitably disposed of, and that the repeated rejection of the grant has not been dictated by a sound and liberal policy." For the procedure followed by the government, see the *Journal of the House of Assembly of New Brunswick,* 1837, pp 249, 326, 392. In 1842 the Baptist Education Society pleaded for government support on two grounds: the usefulness of the institution, and the "large amount of personal sacrifices which have been made for its establishment and support." See *Messenger and Visitor,* April 15, 1842, p. 113.

26   Levy, "The New Brunswick Baptist Seminary," p. 3 (115).

27   Katherine MacNaughton, *The Development of Higher Education in New Brunswick* (Fredericton: U.N.B. Historical Studies, No. 1, 1947), p. 100: "The granting of provincial aid to this school [the New Brunswick Baptist Seminary] seems to have set a kind of precedent for legislative aid to denominational schools other than Anglican. Evidently the Baptists had had to fight custom and Church of England monopoly in order to get the financial support they finally did receive...." She notes that Baptists in 1839 were complaining about the injustice of denying their modest requests for grants when the province was annually bestowing £2,200 on King's College although it was Episcopalian and £400 a year on the Madras Schools although they taught the Anglican Catechism. Cf. Bill, *op. cit.,* p. 323: "There had been a struggle between sectarian exclusiveness and oppression on the one hand and a determination to enjoy equal rights on the other. The conflict was sharp, but in the issue the right prevailed. As one of the most important results of that struggle, instead of King's College, Fredericton, with its ecclesiastical tests bristling on all sides, we have now the University of New Brunswick, established on a broad

and liberal basis, open to all alike."

28 *Minutes of the N.B.B.A.,* Salisbury, 1836, p. 7. The second Annual Report of the N.B.B.E.S. noted the wide appeal of the academy: "There have been about seventy young persons in attendance, since the commencement of the school, the parents of whom are to be found among the members of almost all the religious denominations in the province; nearly one half of that number were from different parts of the province, and boarded in the Seminary."

29 In its Annual Report for 1838, the N.B.B.E.S. paid tribute to the contribution of Mrs. Miles, remarking that the young ladies in the province received from her "the most valuable religious, moral, literary and polite instructions." *(Minutes of the N.B.B.A.,* Springfield, 1838, p. 20). Charlotte Mears Miles was born at Boston, Mass., on May 20, 1812 and died on December 10, 1837. She is buried with her husband in the old Loyalist Cemetery between Brunswick and George Streets in downtown Fredericton.

30 Miles travelled to England, where he presented the needs of the New Brunswick Baptist Seminary. He spoke at a public meeting of the Baptist Colonial Missionary Society held in London on December 5, 1838, urging the claims of the North American Colonies and observing that the views entertained of them in England were in many respects mistaken. See *Baptist Magazine* (London), 1839, p. 22. According to R.B. Wallace, "Some Historical Data of the Brunswick St. Baptist Church in Fredericton,· January 1814 to 1945," *The Maritime Advocate and Busy East,* Vol. 35, No. 12, July 1945, p. 29, Miles obtained $2000 for the Seminary library in England in 1839. Similarly Saunders, *op. cit.,* p. 235.

31 Dedham, *op. cit.,* pp. 22-23, offers a useful biographical sketch of the elder Tupper, who was the father of Sir Charles Tupper, one of the fathers of Confederation and a Prime Minister of Canada. For further details see Bill, *op cit.,* pp. 681-734. In a letter to *The Christian Messenger,*

November 8, 1839, Principal Tupper mentioned that "several of the dear youth have recently obtained hope in the Saviour." There are similar indications of spiritual quickening scattered throughout the history of the Seminary.

32   *Minutes of the N.B.B.A.,* Fredericton, 1842, p. 26.

33   A plaque in his memory was placed in the old Fredericton Baptist Church where Miles served from 1834 to his death in 1842, but it apparently perished in the fire which demolished the wooden structure in 1881. While "perhaps not the greatest preacher," Jarivs Ring, *op.cit.,* p. 69, spoke of Miles as one of the most devoted, humble and pious ministers "that can be named." He was qualified "to advance the interest of religion and the Baptist cause...." There is a short sketch of Miles' contribution to both the Fredericton Baptist Church and to the Seminary in H.C. Creed, "Brief Historical Sketch of the Baptist Church in Fredericton," in A.U.A., Brunswick St. United Baptist Church Records, Book F, pp. 83-84. Creed recognizes that "the establishment of the New Brunswick Baptist Seminary was largely due to his suggestions and his energetic efforts." *The New Brunswick Royal Gazette,* February 16, 1842, paid Miles this tribute: "He was distinguished as a true friend to his country, and as one whose physical and mental energies were perseveringly exerted to promote its temporal and spiritual interests, and as an eminently holy and useful Minister of the Gospel."

34   *Minutes of the N.B.B.A.,* Hillsborough, 1841, p. 25. This report speaks favorably of Randall's work, noting his "ability and assiduity in the discharge of his duties."

35   *Minutes of the N.B.B.A.,* Fredericton, 1842, p. 26.

36   *Minutes of the N.B.B.A.,* St. Andrews, 1843, p. 21. In reading the minutes of this association meeting pertaining to Randall, one cannot miss the deep feeling of disgust and disappointment which lies behind the N.B.B.E.S.'s statement. On the other hand, A.U.A., Ronald S. Longley, "Horton Academy 1828-1957", T.S.

p. 5, reviews Randall's work at Horton Academy favorably. During his principalship attendance at Horton Academy continued to grow. A.U.A., I.B. Oakes, "History of Horton Academy," TS, 1928, p. 8, adds: "In 1846 he [Randall] was one of the delegates from the Nova Scotia Association to confer with similar delegates from the New Brunswick Association at Saint John to consider the advisability of organizing a Baptist Convention of Nova Scotia, New Brunswick, and Prince Edward Island. The organization was effected at the meeting."

37 *Minutes of the N.B.B.A.,* St. Andrews, 1843, p. 21.

38 *Minutes of the N.B.B.A.,* Fredericton, 1842, p. 26.

39 For the full text of the moving appeal sent out by the Committee of the N.B.B.E.S. see *Baptist Magazine* (London), 1841, pp. 21-22.

40 *Minutes of the N.B.B.A.,* St. Andrews, 1843, p. 22. W. Groser, the Secretary of the Baptist Colonial Missionary Society, wrote on November 17, 1842, to the Committee of Management of the Fredericton Seminary concerning Spurden: "We have received most satisfactory testimonials of his competency and adaptation, from Mr. Crisp, the Theological Tutor of Bristol College; Mr. Huxtable, the Classical Tutor; Mr. Birt, Pastor of the Church at Broadmead, formerly under the care of Mr. Hall; and Mr. Davis, Pastor of the Church at King St., Bristol." (A.U.A. N.B.B.E.S. Records, 1834-1872). A brief but informative account of Spurden's ordination is given in the *Baptist Magazine* (London), 1841, p. 235. In a letter to the Fredericton Baptist Church from Zion Chapel, Hereford, where Spurden had served as pastor before coming to New Brunswick, Reginald Jennings said: "We beg most cordially to recommend him to your entire confidence and esteem, assuring you that during his pastorate and fellowship with us his walk and conversation was in all respects becoming the Gospel of Christ." See A.U.A., Brunswick St. United Baptist

Church Records, Book D. February, 1844, p. 102.

41   Spurden's sterling worth was twice recognized by Acadia, who bestowed on him the honorary degrees of M.A. (1851) and D.D. (1861). For his obituary see Edward Hickson's sketch, *Minutes of the W.N.B.B.A.,* Germain St., Saint John, 1876, pp. 29-30. Hickson noted that Spurden was "a gentleman of good literary attainments, of very fine sensibilities, prudent, wise and modest." He recognized in him "a devoted Christian of exemplary piety", whose "life and teaching have had a salutary influence...." For a similar estimate from the Fredericton Baptist Church see A.U.A., Brunswick St. United Baptist Church Records, Book E, pp. 58-9, memorial tribute by A.F. Randolph and C.L. Hartt. "Of his preaching it is but right to say that, for clearness of statement, for conclusiveness of argument and for elegance of style, his sermons had merit that is rarely equalled." See also the tribute of Bill, *op. cit,* p. 334 and W.E. McIntyre, *Messenger and Visitor,* February 6, 1893, p. 3. A sample of Spurden's sermons appears in his Circular Letter to the Churches prepared for the Western Association meeting at St. George *(Minutes of the W.N.B.B.A.,* 1868, pp. 13-15). It is evangelical, calvinistic, practical and biblical. See also Spurden's paper on *Materialism Not A Doctrine of Scripture* (Fredericton, 1867), 22 pp., the Legislative Library, Fredericton, N.B. According to information contained in a letter from C. Sidney Hall, Secretary of Bristol Baptist College to the author, dated June 20, 1979, "Spurden entered Bristol College from the Church in London known as Salter's Hall in 1836. We have no details of his time at college. At that time our students did not take a degree, unless they proceeded to a Scottish university. Spurden went to the pastorate at Hereford when he left here. A history of the Hereford Baptist Church written by H.A. Neal in 1978 says he was inducted to the pastorate on April 13, 1841. His successor arrived in April 1844...."

42　According to a letter from John T. Smith, Secretary of the N.B.B.E.S., dated Fredericton, March 28, 1843, "the school will probably not be what we wish it to be for some time, having been a good deal broken up by change of teachers after the Rev. Mr. Miles' death." *(Baptist Magazine*, 1843, p. 261). The letter spoke favorably of Mr. Spurden's reception in Fredericton, and pleaded for help from England for the establishement of a "respectable library." This appeal for books was repeated in April 1854, when Spurden wrote to the Baptist Missionary Society and to his personal friends for help *(Baptist Magazine* , 1854, p. 351). The curriculum in 1849 is revealed in the following advertisement which appeared in *The Christian Visitor*, March 9, 1849, p. 64: "The studies are conducted under the inspection of the Principal, and comprise English Grammar, Reading, Writing, etc., English Composition, Ancient and Modern History, Geography, the Latin and Greek Languages, Arithmetic, Book Keeping, Algebra, Geometry, Trigonometry, Surveying, Navigation, Natural Philosophy, etc." An excellent description of a typical examination at the Seminary is given by I.E. Bill in *The Christian Visitor*, June 15, 1849, p. 170.

43　The Committee of Management in its Annual Report to the Western Association commented on "the ability and zeal manifested by Mr. Munro in advancing the interests of the Academy, and the efficient aid he has rendered in the discipline and moral culture of the students, and especially his devotedness in affording spiritual instruction and guidance to the young men of the institution." *(Minutes of the W.N.B.B.A.,* Carleton, Saint John, 1855, p. 20). His influence over the students who boarded with him in the house was termed "highly beneficial."

44　On his year as Principal see Isaiah Wallace, *Autobiographical Sketch with Reminiscences of Revival Work* (Halifax: John Burgoyne, n.d.), pp. 27-28.

45　For the Committee of Management's tribute to Day see

the Annual Report of the N.B.B.E.S. in *Minutes of the W.N.B.B.A.,* Fredericton, 1859, Appendix, p. 2.

46　*The Christian Visitor,* June 14, 1866, p. 2. Philip Allwood, "Elevating the Standard: The Fredericton Seminary," *op.cit.,* p. 15 (35), ignores the fact that Spurden resigned as Principal in 1866, and J.E. Hopper succeeded him. That this arrangement was put into practice is indicated by an advertisement in *The Christian Visitor,* September 6, 1866, p. 3, where Spurden is listed as "Professor of Theology and Hebrew" and J.E. Hopper, A.B., is listed as "Principal and Classical and Mathematical Tutor."

47　*Minutes of the W.N.B.B.A.,* Saint John, 1867, p. 38. For a similar estimate see the comments of W.E. McIntyre, *Messenger and Visitor,* February 6, 1893, p. 3: "To this [school], which he loved and for which he prayed and labored with unswerving fidelity, he gave the lifeblood of his Christian manhood, stamping upon its work ineffaceable marks of his own sterling Christian character."

48　In an anonymous account of the "History of the Union St. United Baptist Church" (1929), in A.U.A. p. 1, Dr. Hopper is described as "a man of great intellect and spiritual power." He visited St. Stephen in the summer of 1869, "preached in Mark's Hall, Water St., and arranged to take charge of the few Baptists." He also organized a Sunday School, and a church building was completed on January 7, 1870 and the Church was then duly organized with a membership of 17. For a more comprehensive history of the Union St. Baptist Church see, *A Century of Christian Adventure (1869-1969).* For references to Dr. Hopper note pp. 2-4, 5-6. Prior to his departure for St. Stephen, Hopper had served as pastor of the Queen St. Baptist Church in Fredericton as well as Principal of the Seminary. The Queen St. Church was reunited with the Fredericton Baptist Church in 1869. See H. Gertrude Davis, *The History of Brunswick Street United Baptist Church* (Fredericton, 1964), p. 10. Hopper's service was recognized when the Committee of Management commended him "for the ability, fidelity, and earnestness which you have brought, so successfully, to bear upon the interests committed to your trust" *(Minutes of the W.N.B.B.A.,* Blissfield, Miramichi, p. 1869, p. 36).

49 See Watson Kirkconnell, (ed.) *The Acadia Record 1838-1953* (Wolfville, 1953), p. 495, which also notes that Professor Wortman was awarded an honorary M.A. in 1884.

50 For a brief biographical sketch of Dr. Goodspeed's career see W.S. Wallace, *The Dictionary of Canadian Biography,* (Toronto, 1963), I, 236. Goodspeed, who studied at U.N.B. , Newton Theological Seminary, and Leipzig University, served as editor of the *Messenger and Visitor* (1885-90), and as President of the Maritime Baptist Convention in 1890, and later became Professor of Systematic Theology and Apologetics at McMaster University (1891-1905), and at Baylor University, Waco, Texas (1905-09). He wrote one book, *The Messiah's Second Advent* (Toronto, 1900), and was honored by both Acadia (M.A., 1870; D.D., 1889) and U.N.B. (LL.D., 1900). He was undoubtedly one of the most distinguished graduates of the New Brunswick Baptist Seminary. Goodspeed is listed in W.E. McIntyre, *Manual of Baptist Authors,* typescript in Acadia University Library, Wolfville, N.S., Vol. 4, no page cited. McIntyre notes that Goodspeed was ordained in Andover, N.B. in 1869, studied also at Regent's Park College, London, and died at Paradise, N.S. on July 12, 1912. The correct date of his death is really July 6, 1912, for his obituary appears in *The Canadian Baptist* (July 18, 1912). Apparently McIntyre mistook the notice of death for the date of death. For two moving tributes to Dr. Goodspeed by W.E. Norton see *The McMaster University Monthly,* Jan. 1906, pp. 145-151 and Feb., 1913, pp. 199-206. In a letter in the Canadian Baptist Archives, Hamilton, Ont., Goodspeed to Dr. O.C.S. Wallace, Aug. 13, 1900, Dr. Goodspeed gave his considered opinion that selfish motives lay behind the re-establishment of the seminary in

Saint John rather than unifying all educational work at Acadia: "I do not wish to judge, but I have no doubt but that jealousy of Nova Scotia and want of sympathy for Acadia were the deepest reasons for the course taken."

51 *Minutes of the Eastern New Brunswick Baptist Association* (hereafter referred to as E.N.B.B.A.), Hopewell, 1872, p. 7. It is interesting to note that the preservation of the Wolfville institutions was mentioned. as one of the major reasons for closing the Fredericton Academy. So the Eastern Association wrestled with the decision, pondering "whether to continue the Seminary on its present footing by concentrating our efforts solely towards its support, and thereby incur the very probable risk of the shutting up of Acadia College, or to consolidate all our exertions in the sustaining of the Academy and College at Wolfville."

52 A.U.A., N.B.B.E.S. Records, July 26, 1872, and *Minutes of the E.N.B.B.A.,* Cambridge, 1873, p. 36.

53 A.U.A., N.B.B.E.S. Records, July 26, 1872. Spurden was given the task of "instructing young men who have the ministry in view, and fitting them as far as possible for that work, and also preparing such young men as may desire it for the Training School, and for Acadia College." Cf. A.U.A., N.B.B.E.S. Records, June 6, 1867, which make similar reference to the Committee of Management's earlier decision that "the Theological Department be placed under the control of Rev. Dr. C. Spurden, his salary to be paid by the Denomination."

54 The Principal reported that "thirteen students have entered the Seminary, four of whom declared their intention to enter the ministry; one of these, however, withdrew immediately, on account of ill health, and another for want of means; five were preparing for College; one of whom entered Acadia College last January; three were fitting themselves to enter the Training School; and one was preparing for a profession." *Minutes of the E.N.B.B.A.,* Cambridge, 1873, p. 36; also *Minutes of the W.N.B.B.A.,* Keswick, 1873, p. 44.

55 *Minutes of the W.N.B.B.A.,* Keswick, 1873, p. 8. Similarly, *Minutes of the E.N.B.B.A.,* Cambridge, 1873, pp. 35-36.

56 *Minutes of the E.N.B.B.A.,* Elgin, 1874, p. 32. Cf. Bill, *op. cit.,* p. 621. *The New Brunswick Board of Education, 1873 Report,* City of Fredericton section, reported the sale of the Seminary building. The 1874 Report noted that the building was occupied towards the end of April 1874 by the six classes which formerly assembled in the Orange Hall. At Elgin it was noted that "it was decided at the Annual Meeting of the N.B.B.E.S. held in connection with the W.N.B.B.A. at Jacksonville, Carleton Co. on June 24, 1874, that the Bond of School Trustees for $5,000 be deposited in the Bank of New Brunswick, Saint John, in the name of the Western and Eastern Associations." See also the N.B.B.E.S. Report for 1874, *The Baptist Year Book of Nova Scotia, New Brunswick, and Prince Edward Island,* p. 42, which reports the sale of the Seminary's physical assets. *The New Brunswick Board of Education, 1889 Report,* noted the "dilapidated condition" of the old Seminary building which made it "very difficult to carry on the work there in a satisfactory manner." In 1891 tenders were invited for the removal of the old building to the northwest corner of the playground. The contract was awarded to Mr. Andrew Johnston of Saint John. This difficult job was carried out on June 23, 1891, according to the 1891 Report. In 1892 York Street School was still located in the old Seminary building, but the 1893 Report announced the completion of the new school building "in which the Grammer School is conveniently located." The old Seminary building was subsequently torn down. In 1926 the Fredericton High School building was ready for occupancy, and the York St. School reverted to an elementary school building until 1965, when it was purchased by its neighbour, the Brunswick St. United Baptist Church.

57 Among them were Calvin Goodspeed, J.E.P. Hopper, A.H. Munro, Judson Blakeney, Joseph Blakeney, Peter

McLeod, W.A. Coleman, Robert Mutch, Benjamin N. Hughes, Benjamin Jewett, John Magee and R.H. Emmerson. Calvin Goodspeed's contribution to McMaster University is reviewed by Charles M. Johnson, *McMaster University* (Toronto, 1976), I, 66, 90. He is praised in official McMaster minutes for his "faithful, self-sacrificing work" and recognized by the Senate as a "tower of strength against immature and erroneous teaching." The Rev. W.A. Coleman, according to Saunders *op. cit.*, pp. 477, "was ordained in 1845 at North Esk; baptized 1,050 during his life; he was a wise counsellor and sound preacher, and was zealous in all good works." Saunders, *op.cit.,* pp. 486, 487, 489f. also has brief notes on Hughes ("He was a successful pastor"), Jewett ("He was an earnest preacher") and Magee ("He was pastor of the church at Nashwaak when his health failed.") According to Emmerson Carroll and A. Joyce Tingley, *Years of Pilgrimage — 150 Years for Christ in the First Moncton United Baptist Church* (Hantsport, N.S., 1978), p. 23, R.H. Emmerson was one of the early pastors of the First Baptist Church, Moncton, N.B.: "He was the second native-born New Brunswicker to minister to the Baptist Fellowship in Moncton. Trained at the Fredericton Baptist Seminary and Acadia, he was a born orator and leader of men. While he had attractive offers to pulpits in the United States, he felt compelled to serve the churches of his native province." Unfortunately his ministry in Moncton was but a year and eleven days (September 1856-September 1857), for "he contracted typhoid fever and died very suddenly."

58 Creed, *A Baptist Academy for New Brunswick,* p. 5. Another aspect not mentioned by Creed should be noted, namely, the contribution of the New Brunswick Baptist Seminary to the teaching profession. The Annual Report of the N.B.B.E.S. for 1839, for instance, observed that "no less than eight young persons of good moral character and habits had, at that time been qualified at the Seminary as Parish School Teachers, had passed the Board of

Examination as by law instituted, obtained licences, and were teaching Schools in different parts of the Province, where, in some cases, no Schools had been before taught." *(Minutes of the N.B.B.A.,* Springfield, 1839).

59 The controversy between H.C. Creed and J.E. Hopper over reopening the New Brunswick Baptist Seminary is reflected very vividly in *The Christian Visitor*, November 22, 1881, p. 4. See also Creed, *op. cit.,* p. 5: "Many felt it to be a heavy burden. It only needed the establishment of the Free School System to lead thoughtful men to the belief that the usefulness of the Seminary was at an end. They concluded that there was no longer need of a Baptist academy in this Province." Cf. *Minutes of the W.N.B.B.A.,* Fredericton, 1872, p. 11, which suggested that the only real alternative to the continuance of the Seminary was "to unite with our Nova Scotia brethren in academic as well as·collegiate and theological education, and concentrate all our efforts with a view to the greatest possible efficiency of Acadia as the single educational centre of the Baptists of the three provinces." See also *The Christian Visitor,* August 9, 1882, p. 4, which speaks of serious legal opposition to the reopening of the Seminary in Saint John on the part of Mr. R.H. Phillips of Fredericton. The disposal of the Seminary's invested funds was another bone of contention. Some advocated the use of the money for the Wolfville institutions, while others insisted that it be used for the advancement of higher education in New Brunswick.

60 *Minutes of the W.N.B.B.A.,* Rockland, 1879, in the report of J.F. Burditt.

61 *Minutes of the E.N.B.B.A.,* Harvey, 1881, p. 21. This report, the minutes add, was "somewhat inharmoniously but vigorously discussed" by Brethren Gates, Hopper, Everett, Knapp, and afterwards adopted. This is a striking instance of the associational principle in action.

62 *Minutes of the Southern New Brunswick Baptist*

Association (hereafter referred to as S.N.B.B.A.), St. George, 1882, Appendix, p. 1. Bannister, *op. cit.,* p. 4, cites a similar resolution passed by the Western Association which met that year at Richmond, Carleton Co.

63 *Minutes of the E.N.B.B.A.,* Havelock, 1882, pp. 8-9: "Whereas the New Brunswick Baptist Education Society was organized to provide Education under Christian watchcare, and as there is at this day pressing necessity for the work, therefore (be it) resolved that we recommend the Society to make provisions at an early day for the reopening of the Baptist Seminary." The Report on Education delivered at the Eastern Association's 1880 meeting has supported Wolfville rather than Saint John as the proper Baptist educational centre: "No Provincial lines or sectional boundaries should in our regard be attached to the Institutions at Wolfville. They are *ours* to cherish in our hearts, and to sustain by our confidence, our prayers, our beneficence, and by the patronage of our sons and daughters." *(Minutes of the E.N.B.B.A.,* Sackville, 1880.)

64 See Kirkconnell, *The Acadia Record,* p. 15, for biographical details of McVicar's interesting career. Among other educational achievements, he authored two books: a *Short History of Annapolis* and *Imperial Britain.* Levy, *The Baptists of the Maritime Provinces,* p. 217, mistakenly lists Dr. Hopper as the Principal of the new school in Saint John. This assertion, however, is explicitly contradicted by a detailed news report in *The Daily Telegraph,* Saint John, N.B., June 23, 1883, p. 3, which correctly identifies the incoming Principal as W.M. McVicar. So also does Bannister, *op. cit.,* p. 5.

65 See *"The Baptist Seminary," The Christian Visitor,* December 27, 1882, p. 4. This article also mentions a music-room and a studio, and speaks of "ample accommodation for 100 students." See also *The Christian Visitor,* September 20, 1882, p. 4. Saint John had been advocated as the proper location as far back as 1857, when

a special committee reported that "there is in that city and its vicinity a population amply sufficient to sustain a first-class Seminary in a high state of efficiency." *(Minutes of the W.N.B.B.A.,* Nashwaak, 1857, p. 9.)

66 *The Daily Sun,* Saint John, May 23, 1883, p. 186. An advertisement in *The Christian Visitor,* December 20, 1882, p. 2, stressed the advantages of the new school: "Excellent facilities are here afforded for pursuing a classical course preparatory to College or Professional work. Young ladies or gentlemen who may wish to study for a Provincial license, or who may desire thorough and efficient instruction to prepare for Commercial pursuits will find this institution suited to their requirements."

67 *The Daily Telegraph,* Saint John, June 23, 1883, p. 3.

68 Cf. The *Minutes of the New Brunswick Free Christian Baptist General Conference* (hereafter referred to as N.B.F.C.B.G.C.), Tracy's Mills, October 1894, p. 44. "It was...during the Conference of 1883 that we decided, conjointly with our Baptist brethren, to undertake the control of the Union Baptist Seminary."

69 *The Christian Visitor,* October 31, 1883, p. 4: *Minutes of the N.B.F.C.B.G.C.,* Tracy's Mills, 1883, p. 47. On the government of the Union Baptist Seminary see *Messenger and Visitor,* October 7, 1891, p. 4.

70 *Union Baptist Seminary Calendar 1894-95,* cited by Bannister, *op. cit.,* p. 5. For the statistics for 1884 see *Minutes of the E.N.B.B.A.,* Dorchester, 1884, p. 45. That year there were 100 students: "Of these 13 were studying with a view to the Ministry; 8 young ladies graduated, 7 have prepared to matriculate at College and several more are studying with that aim."

71 For a detailed description and a large photograph of "the new institution on Lancaster Heights" see *The Daily Sun,* Saint John, January 7, 1885.

72 *The Seminary Bema,* April 1893, p. 67, cited by Bannister, *op. cit.,* p. 6.

73 *Minutes of the N.B.F.C.B.G.C.,* Carleton, Saint John,

October 9-13, 1886, p. 48.

74   H.H. Mott, a Saint John architect, was then in the early stages of a brilliant fifty year career. Among other buildings which he designed were the Grand Hotel, Yarmouth, Baptist churches in Yarmouth, Amherst and Saint John (Main St.), Harkins Academy, Newcastle and Enterprise Foundry, Sackville, N.B. Interestingly, he married Hattie N. Hopper, daughter of Dr. J.E. Hopper, who was to serve as Principal of the St. Martins Seminary from 1889 to 1892. For more details see C.H. McLean, *Prominent People of New Brunswick* (n.p., 1937), p. 65.

75   *Messenger and Visitor,* July 21, 1886, cited by Bannister, *op. cit.,* p. 6. For an informative description of "The Seminary as a School and Home" see *The Seminary Bema,* February 1890, p. 1.

76   *The Union Baptist Seminary Calendar for 1892-93, p. 9f.* Similarly *Minutes of the N.B.F.C.B.G.C.,* Midland, October 1-5, 1887, p. 49: "The location is beautiful for situation, and finer structures for educational purposes, or a better system for heating and ventilation is not to be found in the Maritime Provinces." For a detailed description of the premises see *The Daily Sun,* Saint John, July 21, 1886. Briefly, the central section contained the Principal's apartments, reading hall, classrooms, music rooms, chapel and dining room. The right and left wings were occupied by the young men and the young women respectively. They housed both the students' dormitories and teachers' apartments. There were bathrooms in each flat and in every department, furnished with hot and cold water. The heating and ventilating were sophisticated, making use of the Smead-Dowd system.

77   *The Seminary Bema,* April 1893, p. 68, cited by Bannister, *op.cit.,* p. 6.

78   B.F. Simpson's career is outlined in Saunders, *op. cit.,* p. 501: "He was born in Prince Edward Island in 1854; graduated Acadia College, 1880, and at Morgan Park Theological Seminary, 1882 (B.D.). He held three pastorates in the United States; was principal for one year

of St. Martins Seminary (1888-89); pastor at South Berwick, Maine, for three years, and assistant professor of theology in the University of Chicago. He died in 1894."

79   For helpful sketches of John Elias Peck Hopper, D.D., see Kirkconnell, *op.cit.,* p. 8 and G.M. Rose, (ed.), *A Cyclopaedia of Canadian Biography* (Toronto, 1888), pp. 336-37. In addition to the pastoral charge of the Brussels St. Baptist Church in Saint John, Dr. Hopper published in the 1880's *The Christian Visitor, Canadian Record, Youth's Visitor, Gem and The International Sunday School Lessons.* Saunders, *op. cit.,* p. 486, comments: "He was an able preacher and educator."

80   In a general circular letter to the Baptist churches of New Brunswick (ca. June 1890), the financial needs of the Seminary were placed squarely before the constituency: "The great hindrance to the highest usefulness of the school now is the debt on the property. We can fill the building with students, and we can pay all current expenses from receipts. We are pressed, however, for payment of bills contracted in securing this grand educational centre.'

81   *The Seminary Bema,* April 1893, p. 68. Cf. *Messenger and Visitor,* December 23, 1891, p. 4.

82   *Messenger and Visitor,* March 30, 1892, p. 4.

83   For a useful biographical sketch see Kirkconnell, *op. cit.,* pp. 29-30. On Dr. de Blois' great contribution to Eastern Baptist Theological Seminary in Philadelphia (1926-36) see Gordon H. Baker, "The Formative Years," *What God Hath Wrought,* (ed.) Gilbert L. Guffin (Philadelphia, 1960), pp. 55-73; cf. also Norman H. Maring, "Conservative But Progressive," *What God Hath Wrought,* pp. 41-43. When Dr. de Blois retired in 1936 the Board of Trustees paid tribute to his outstanding contribution: "His scholarly habits and attainments, his fine teaching ability, his strong conservative convictions, his vigorous and aggressive spirit, his far-reaching vision, his strong grasp of modern problems, his success as an author, his achievements as editor of the *Christian*

Review, his splendid contacts with the colleges and with the denomination, have qualified Dr. de Blois for the roll of honor, and have placed Eastern Seminary in his debt forever." (Baker, "The Formative Years", p. 73.)

84 *Baptist Year Book,* 1892, p. 102, cited by Bannister, *op. cit.,* p. 7. For a useful summary of the events of the academic year 1891-92 see *Minutes of the N.B.F.C.B.G.C.,* Corn Hill, Kings Co., October 1892, pp. 28-29.   For the following year see *Minutes of the N.B.F.C.B.G.C.,* Saint John, October 1893, pp. 32-33, which describes the 1892-93 year as "a period of unqualified success," but recognizes that "another resolute effort is needed in order to free us from this incubus (of debts), which has perplexed us for so long."

85 *Messenger and Visitor,* June 21, 1893, p. 4.

86 Bannister, *op. cit.,* p. 7, cites an interesting statement Dr. de Blois once made: "I wish it to be distinctly understood, however, that the fundamental aim of the school will ever be to direct the footsteps of students towards Acadia, since it cannot be doubted that in our day a college training is the fittest preparation for any calling in life." (*The Seminary Bema,* April 1893, p. 70). This statement also appears in *Messenger and Visitor,* May 4, 1892, p. 4.

87 *Union Baptist Seminary Calendar,* 1892-93, p. 12.

88 *Ibid.* The English-Scientific Course gave special attention to the branches indicated in its name and substituted "certain studies in Science for the languages of the Classical Course."

89 The original Constitution of the N.B.B.E.S. adopted in 1833 had laid down in Article 12 that tuition and board were "to be fixed at as low a rate as possible." See *The Christian Visitor,* January 18, 1866, p. 2. In 1836, for example, the fees for tuition and board were 7 shillings 6 pence per week, or £16.10.0 per year, making allowance of the deduction of the eight week vacation. The whole expense for tuition, board, lodging and washing came to £19.10.0 at the lowest, and £21.10.0 at the highest, per

annum. There was also a charge of 5 shillings for fuel for each of the winter terms (*Minutes of the N.B.B.A.,* Salisbury, 1836, p. 8). The students were required to furnish their own bedding, towel, books, stationery, etc.

90 Bannister, *op. cit.,* p. 8.

91 *Union Baptist Seminary Calendar,* 1893-94, p. 23 cited by Bannister, *op. cit.,* p. 8. For an informative report of the closing exercises for 1893 see *Messenger and Visitor,* June 21, 1893, p. 4. After mentioning the Eclectic Society's meeting on Saturday night the Calendar concluded: "The social life is genial and helpful in a high degree, while the friendships formed are often a source of delight and satisfaction when the happy school days are ended."

92 *Union Baptist Seminary Calendar,* 1892-93, pp. 17, 19, 24. In addition, the students published a sixteen-page literary periodical called *The Seminary Bema.*

93 Bannister *op.cit.,* p. 9. Dr. Hopper wrote: "...our endeavour is to bring all under such Christian influence that by God's blessing all talents of every class may be laid upon the altar and used to promote the name that is above every name." *(Messenger and Visitor,* April 1, 1891, Supplement, no page cited). See also the remarks of Dr. de Blois at the Western New Brunswick Baptist Association in Fredericton in *Messenger and Visitor,* July 6, 1892, p. 1. A little later Dr. de Blois, speaking at the General Convention meeting in Bridgewater, N.S., in 1892, noted that fine educational advantages were offered at St. Martins, but "it is desired especially that Christ may reign in the hearts of the students. The vexing and disturbing social and political questions that are reaching us must be answered by men and women educated and trained under Christian influence. The evil things in this world must be met and conquered by the power of the Holy Ghost....It is the power of the Holy Ghost that we need in our schools." Similarly the Free Baptists commended the school "both for its educational advantages...and for its sweet Christian atmosphere." *(Minutes of the N.B.F.C.B.G.C.,* St. John , 1893, p. 32)

Cf. also *Messenger and Visitor,* July 6, 1892, p. 1, where Dr. de Blois "emphasized the value of physical culture, but still more strongly that of moral and spiritual teaching and influence."

94   *Union Baptist Seminary Calendar,* 1893-94, p. 25, cited by Bannister, *op. cit.,* p. 9. See also the *Union Baptist Seminary Calendar,* 1892-93, which stressed the Seminary's emphasis on character formation, its endorsement of co-education "within reasonable limits and with certain definite and positive restrictions", its wholesome and uplifting home atmosphere, and its advocacy of gymnastics and physical education. Dr. de Blois during dark days said: "...we had resolved with each other, and with the help of God, to make our school a power in the land." He enlisted others to "join with us earnestly and zealously in our efforts to build a Christian school that shall be a centre of force and influence." *(Messenger and Visitor,* July 13, 1892, p. 4.)

95   Note the student comment in *The Seminary Bema,* February 1890, p. 1: "The students are highly favored in regard to privileges, of which we have many, much greater freedom being allowed here than in similar institutions." However, the students who produced the literary magazine were themselves strongly opposed to certain habits. They described smoking, for example, as an "evil habit" and found the use of tobacco to be "an offensive, disgusting, hurtful, and degrading habit." *(The Seminary Bema,* May 1890, p. 61).

96   *Union Baptist Seminary Calendar,* 1892-93, p. 19.

97   *Union Baptist Seminary Calendar,* 1892-93, p. 19. The students themselves recognized the value of "Earnestness," *The Seminary Bema,* November 1893, p. 89. For the regulations of the Baptist Seminary in Fredericton see *Minutes of the W.N.B.B.A.,* Jacksontown, 1856, p. 30.

98   See, for example, C.H. Day, "A Visit to St. Martins Seminary," *Messenger and Visitor,* May 1893, no page

cited. Dr. de Blois wrote a year later in a similar vein: "The Lord has been with us, and we have prospered, beyond my expectations. Additions and improvements have been made and paid for....The interest on the mortgage is paid to this date. Our building is filled to overflowing. The students are as bright and earnest and noble a company of young people as one will find anywhere. The moral and religious influences are stimulating. The teaching-staff is composed of men and women of high Christian character, who are splendidly equipped for their work." *(Messenger and Visitor,* March 21, 1894, p. 4). See also *The Seminary Bema,* April 1893, p. 71.

99 Financial burdens were bearing heavily upon the institution, and there was the fear that they might crush it in 1891 when under pressure from certain creditors an assignment had been made to Jacob S. Titus of St. Martins *(Messenger and Visitor,* May 13, 1891, p. 4). For details see *Minutes of the N.B.F.C.B.G.C.,* Marysville, 1891, p. 40, and the report by A. K. de Blois, *Messenger and Visitor,* November 18, 1891, p. 5. This crisis was met successfully. However, on March 21, 1894, there appeared an advertisement in the *Messenger and Visitor* (p. 3) to sell St. Martins Seminary. The sale was subject to a mortgage of $10,000, and possession was to be given by July 1, 1894. In July of that year Dr. de Blois reported to the Southern Association meeting at St. Croix that the school was in danger of being closed *(Messenger and Visitor,* July 18, 1894, p. 1). In answer to a question put by a member of the association it was stated that the debt on the Seminary was about $28,000. Dr. de Blois stated his reasons for resignation in a moving letter to the *Messenger and Visitor,* March 21, 1894, p. 4. For further financial details of the debt see *Messenger and Visitor,* June 27, 1894, p. 4. In the *Messenger and Visitor,* December 26, 1894, p. 4, the new Principal W.E. McIntyre sadly reported: "Owing to certain difficulties in connection with the property, and also owing partly to the great expense incurred in the management of the school,

we have decided to abandon the Seminary building for the winter. The class, however, will be continued in the residence of the late Captain Wishart, a large and commodious edifice sufficient for the present wants of the school. Here a comfortable home will be furnished for the young men, while young ladies attending will be placed in approved families in the village."

100   The Report of the Committee on Education of the Free Christian Baptists, for instance, admitted in October 5, 1896: "That we have now not even a connection or interest in any institution of learning is a matter of profound regret" (*Minutes of the N.B.F.C.B.G.C.,* Victoria St., Saint John, 1896, p.33). The report does not spell out the details of the school's demise. The deathknoll had sounded. The Seminary was no more.

101   *The Minutes of the New Brunswick Baptist Convention* (N.B.B.C.), Jemseg, September 8-11, 1894, p. 10, record the resolution that the New Brunswick Baptist Convention "offer to the Free Christian Baptist Conference of New Brunswick the following proposition, namely: That of the amount required to purchase St. Martins Seminary we agree to raise two-thirds, provided that the Free Christian Baptists raise one-third, taking therewith a proportional share of the ownership and control of the institutions." Reading between the lines, one gets the impression that the Free Christian Baptists were finding the original 50/50 arrangement a heavy burden in the face of the institution's increasing debt. This impression is confirmed when the Committee on Education of the Free Baptists reported a month later *(Minutes of the N.B.F.C.B.G.C.,* Tracy's Mills, October 13-17, 1894, p. 44): "...we have reached a crisis....The history of that institution during those years is a disastrous one, and need not be minutely described here....It will be the duty of this Conference to consider carefully and wisely the present aspect of the Seminary and our relation thereto. In the unsettled condition of affairs in connection with

this institution your Committee cannot do other than request this Conference to consider whether, — 1. We shall make an effort to maintain a connection with the school or not. 2. As to our share of the present indebtedness of the $12,000, which we are morally bound to pay." The Committee closed its report by urging that "something definite should be done to place our educational work on a better basis." In February 1895 the Free Baptists "announced their decision to withdraw from any share in the control of the school." They indicated, however, their desire to assist in paying off the debt. See *Messenger and Visitor*, September 25, 1895, p. 4.

102 *Messenger and Visitor*, June 27, 1894, p. 2. G.W. Titus, a local merchant of St. Martins, is plainly described in the *Messenger and Visitor* as "the present owner of the Seminary building and lands." He was reputed to have a "deep interest" in the Seminary, and was anxious to help it out of its financial difficulties. Significantly, the *New Brunswick Baptist Annual* of 1896 makes no mention of St. Martins Seminary, although it mentions Acadia College (120 students), Horton Academy (88), and Acadia Seminary (110).

103 See *Messenger and Visitor,* July 4, 1894, p. 4, which gives detailed information on the financial position of the Union Baptist Seminary.

104 *Minutes of the S.N.B.B.A.,* Hampton Village, 1896, p. 22. Cf. E.R. Fitch, ed. *The Baptists of Canada* (Toronto, 1911), p. 84. He adds: "It did a valuable work for the Baptists of New Brunswick and for public education in that province."

105 Mrs. W.E. Skillen, (ed.), *St. Martins-by-the Sea,* (Saint John, 1898), pp. 40-41. The officers of the Society included F.W. Clark, President and General Manager, and J. Harry King, Secretary. The brochure announced that "a live company has been incorporated and has taken over the magnificent Seminary property...The company owns 200 acres of land with the building, well

adapted for Golf Links and all outdoor sports." (p. 41).

106 Bannister, *op. cit.,* p. 10.

107 An article in *The Evening Times-Globe* of Saint John dated Friday, March 26, 1971, raised questions about the safety of the Seminary building. The Quaco Historical and Library Society was founded in September 1971 in an attempt to save the old building (although it was not incorporated until January 1977). This Society opposed the decision of the provincial government to demolish the old St. Martins School. See *The Evening Times-Globe,* February 14, 1973. However, the school was said to be a fire hazard, and this was a concern to the village council, according to St. Martins Mayor Byard Mora *(The Evening Times-Globe,* February 16, 1973). Shortly thereafter the building was set on fire in the spring and levelled to the ground.

108 Note *The Christian Visitor,* October 31, 1883, p. 5, where I.E. Bill in a letter to the editor views "union in educational work" as a first step toward a more general union of the Baptists and Free Christian Baptists. The same letter appeared also in the *Religious Intelligencer,* November 9, 1883, p. 2. Cf. also Bill's letter to the *Religious Intelligencer,* November 23, 1883, p. 2, which echoes similar thoughts: "Shall those who agree in all that is really essential be kept apart by questions of comparatively small import? Let brotherly love be our guiding star, and we shall soon see the two branches of the Baptist household working together in the bonds of an undying fellowship."

109 Wilma Holland, "History of St. Martins, N.B., 1796-1970." TS, the Quaco Historical and Library Society, St. Martins, N.B., p. 6. St. Martins was the terminus of a branch railway line which ran from Hampton. What it needed was a substantial direct railway service to Saint John. Dorothy F. Smith, "A History of St. Martins, N.B.," TS, the Quaco Historical and Library Society, St. Martins, N.B., incorrectly dates the closing of the Seminary as 1887. The St. Martins Seminary was not

ready for occupancy until 1888!

110   L.E. Wortman studied at the Fredericton Seminary, taught in Saint John, and served as Principal there for three years (1885-1888). Later he was Professor of Modern Languages and History at Acadia University. Sir George Foster, teacher at the Seminary 1870-71, later taught at U.N.B. and served as M.P. and federal Minister of Finance. He was honoured by Acadia (D.C.L.,) 1885. Dr. Case studied at Acadia and Yale, taught mathematics at St. Martins (1893-5), Horton Academy (1895-7), New Hampton, N.H. (1897-1901) and at Cobb Divinity School, Lewiston, Me. (1906-08) before moving on to the University of Chicago for his great lifework in New Testament and early Christian history (1908-38). He died at Lakeland, Florida, Dec. 5, 1947. See Louis B. Jennings, "Shirely Jackson Case," *The Chronicle,* July, 1948, pp. 136-144. Cf. also Massey H. Shepherd Jr's comments in *Criterion,* Autumn, 1978 (vol. 17, no. 3), pp. 23-27.

111   *Minutes of the N.B.B.C.* Havelock, September 10-13, 1898: "To us, as Christians, honor is better than blood." For similar sentiments by Dr. Hopper during the 1891 crisis see *Messenger and Visitor,* June 3, 1891, p. 4: "It will be an everlasting stigma on the Baptist denominations if the property should pass out of our hands and any one be left to say that they had been defrauded out of what was honestly due them." He called upon his fellow Baptists "to save our honor, our honesty, and our Seminary, which is doing for us such a noble Christian work." Cf. also Mrs. William Holland, "St. Martins — The Eventful Story of a Hundred Years," TS, the Quaco Historical and Library Society, St. Martins, N.B., p. 2: "...unless some effort is made to pay off the debt the building will stand here as a monument of the lack of enterprise of the Baptists of the Maritime Provinces."

112   *Messenger and Visitor,* November 15, 1893, p. 2.

113   *Messenger and Visitor,* March 23, 1892, p. 1.

114 *Minutes of the N.B.B.C.,* Haverlock, September 10-13, 1898, p. 54.

115 *Minutes of the N.B.B.C.,* Gibson, York Co., 1897, p. 19.

Alice Shaw and her Grand Pre Seminary: A story of Female Education

1 Lewis Carroll, *Alice in Wonderland,* (New York: J.M. Dent & Sons Ltd., 1977), p. 55.

2 Esther Clark Wright, *Planters and Pioneers* (Hantsport, N.S.: Lancelot Press Ltd., 1978), p. 251.

3 Arthur Wentworth Hamilton Eaton, *History of Kings County* (Salem, Mass.: Salem Press Co., 1910), p. 816.

4 Wright, p. 253.

5 I.E. Bill. *Fifty Years with the Baptist Ministers and Churches of the Maritime Provinces* (Saint John, N.B.: Barnes & Co., 1880), pp. 305-309.

6 Acadia University Archives, Wolfville, N.S. (hereafter A.U.A.), Samual Elder, "Dialogue between Death and a fine young Lady," Mar. 17, 1838, MS.

7 James Bingay, *Public Education in Nova Scotia* (Kingston, Ont.: Jackson Press, 1919) p. 49.

8 A.U.A., Berwick Baptist Church Records, 1829-1858.

9 A.U.A., Alice Shaw Chipman, *Souvenir Scrap Book.*

10 Grace MacLeod Rogers, *Wedge Drives Wedge, address to Acadia Seminary Graduating Class* (n.p. June, 1897), pp. 7,8.

11 "One of the Six." *Messenger and Visitor,*(June 1, 1892),p. 2. These six were the three who began in 1854, also Salome and Hannah Freeman of Harmony who began in 1855, and Lucy Gibbs of Berwick who began in 1856. The latter three stayed one year.

12 *Eighteenth Annual Catalogue of Mount Holyoke Female*

Seminary, 1854-55 (South Hadley, Mass.: Northampton, Hopkins Bridgman & Co., 1855).

13 "One of the six," p. 2.

14 Herbert C. Creed, *A Baptist Academy in New Brunswick* (Fredericton, N.B.: *Daily & Weekly Herald* Office, 1882), p. 5.

15 Irene Elder Morton, *The Acadia Pierian* (Wolfville, N.S.: May, 1905), p. 9.

16 Edward M. Saunders, *History of the Baptists of the Maritime Provinces* (Halifax, N.S.: John Burgoyne, Granville St., 1902), p. 377.

17 T. S. Rand in *The Christian Messenger,* June 18, 1856, p. 197.

18 *The Christian Messenger,* Sept. 30, 1856, p. 286.

19 *The Christian Messenger,* March 4, 1857, p. 61.

20 Saunders, p. 381.

21 *The Christian Messenger,* Aug. 18, 1858, p. 262.

22 *Ibid.*

23 *The Christian Messenger,* Aug. 25, 1858, p. 269.

24 Saunders, p. 381.

25 "Our Village," *The Christian Messenger,* Jan. 14, 1860, p. 29.

26 A.U.A., Alice T. Shaw to Alfred Chipman, n.d. [late 1860].

27 *The Christian Messenger*, Jan. 2, 1861, p. 2.

28 A. C. Boggs, *Story of the Religious Life of Acadia* (Kentville, N.S.: Kentville Pub. Co., 1933), p. 54.

29 A.U.A., Rev. Wm. Chipman, Jan. 23, 1861.

30 Rev. T. H. Higgins in *The Christian Messenger*, Feb. 6, 1861, p. 46.

31 *The Christian Messenger,* July 17, 1861, p. 225.

32 Morton, p. 12.

33 *Ibid.*

34 Mary Nutting, *Historical Sketch of Mount Holyoke*

Seminary (Springfield, Mass.: Clark W. Bryan & Co., 1878), p. 3.

35 A.U.A., MS, Rosina A. Bently Phillips, "Reminiscences of Acadia Ladies Seminary," [probably 1912].

36 Harry Leon McBeth, "Role of Women in Southern Baptist History," *Baptist History and Heritage* (Nashville, Tenn.: Historical Commission, Southern Baptist Convention), Vol. 12, No. 1, Jan., 1977, pp. 3, 4, 19.

37 *Baptist Magazine* (London: T. Smith, Nov. 10, 1810), p. 558.

38 *Canadian Monthly and National Review* (Toronto: Adam, Stevenson & Co., Vol. I, 1872), p. 253.

39 *Journal of Education for Lower Canada* (Montreal: Senecal & Daniel, 1857), p. 114

40 *Canadian Monthly,* p. 252.

41 *The Christian Messenger*, March 16, 1849, pp. 81,82.

42 *Mount Holyoke Annual Catalogue* lists Catharine Lawson (Mrs. John Laurie) of Cornwallis, Kings Co. of the 1850 class, the three girls of 1857, and the two Freeman sisters of Harmony, N.S. These last two attended only one year, but are included along with the three of 1857 by Saunders to comprise the five.

43 Saunders, p. 392.

44 "A Student of '61." *The Christian Messenger,* May 4, 1892, p. 7.

45 Mrs. T. Trotter, "Results of Higher Education of Women," *Acadia Athenaeum* (Wolfville, N.S.: Vol. XXVI, No. 4, Feb. 1900), p. 132.

H.C. Creed, "Record of Graduates in the Years 1865 and 1866," *Memorials of Acadia College and Horton Academy* (Montreal: Dawson Brothers, 1881), p. 176.

Morton, p. 12.

Phillips, pp. 5-7.

Academy Budget, vol. I, No. 5, May 2, 1861, p. 2.

50 Phillips, pp. 13,14.
51 Creed, p. 177.
52 *Budget,* vol. I, no. 1, p. 1.
53 *Budget,* vol. II, No. 5, p. 2.
54 Morton, pp. 14,15.
55 *N.S. Central Association,* 1863, pp. 34, 35.
56 Phillips, p. 1.
57 A.U.A., MS, perhaps by M.R. Eaton, "Chronicles of Acadia Seminary from its Birth."
58 Acadia University, Wolfville, N.S., "Acadia College Governors' Minutes," Dec. , 1870.
59 A.U.A., R.S. Longley, *Horton Academy, 1828-1959,* mimeographed TS, p. 9.
60 "Acadia College Governors' Minutes." 1875.
61 *Baptist Convention Minutes* (Halifax, N.S.: *Christian Messenger* Office, 1877), p. 39.
62 R.S. Longley, *Acadia University, 1838-1938* (Wolfville, N.S., 1939), p. 94.
63 *The Christian Messenger,* Dec. 19, 1877, p. 394.
64 D.G. MacDonald in *The Christian Messenger,* Dec. 19, 1877, p. 402.
65 *The Christian Messenger,* June 11, 1879, p. 186.
66 Longley, *Acadia University,* p. 93.
67 Morton, p. 16.
68 *Baptist Convention Year Book,* 1918, pp. 139, 140.
69 Class Letter to the *Viatoriae* — 1861, 1868, 1887.
70 A.U.A., *Scrap Book,* letter to Acadia Seminary Principal, May 28, 1892.
71 A.U.A., *Scrap Book,* Seminary Jubilee Exercises, May 12, 1892.
72 Used with permission of Trustees of Mount Holyoke College Library/Archives, South Hadley, Mass.
73 *Year Book,* 1921, p. 50.

74 Mrs. Alfred Chipman. "Berwick Baptist Church Diamond Anniversary," in *The Messenger and Visitor,* Nov. 25, 1903, p. 735.

The Union of the Regular and Free Will Baptists of the Maritimes, 1905 and 1906

1 Jarold K. Zeman, *Baptist Roots and Identity* (Brantford, Ontario), 1978, p. 1.

2 *Encyclopaedia Britannica,* 14th Ed. (1939), Vol. 9, p. 622.

3 Norman Baxter, *History of the Free Will Baptists* (Rochester, New York, 1957), preface III.

4 *Ibid.,* pp. 8-18.

5 George E. Levy, *History of the Baptists of the Maritime Provinces* (St. John, N.B., 1946), p. 1.

6 *Ibid.,* p. 10.

7 *Ibid.,* pp. 13 ff.

8 *Ibid.,* p. 33.

9 Edward M. Saunders, *History of the Baptists of the Maritime Provinces* (Halifax, N.S., 1902), p. 21.

10 Reginald S. Dunn, *Union of the Regular and the Free Baptists, 1905-1906* (B. D. Thesis, Acadia, 1941), p. 21.

11 *Ibid.,* p. 22.

12 *The Daily Sun,* St. John, N.B., October 11, 1905 p. 1.

13 *Ibid.,* p. 8

14 *Ibid.,* p. 8

15 *Ibid.,* p. 8

16 *Ibid.,* p. 8

17 *Ibid.,* p. 8

18 *Ibid.,* p. 10

19 *Ibid.,* p. 10

20 *Ibid.*, p. 10

21 *Ibid.*, p. 10; *Minutes of the Free Baptist Conference,* 1903, p. 57.

22 *Minutes of the Free Baptist Conference, 1904.*

23 *The Daily Sun,* p. 10.

24 *Ibid.*, p. 8.

25 *Ibid.*, p. 10.

26 *Ibid.*, p. 1.

27 *Ibid.*, p. 1.

28 Levy, p. 281.

29 *Atlantic United Baptist Convention Year Book,* 1978, Part II, pp. 217-219.

30 Saunders, p. 1.

31 *United Baptist Convention Year Book,* 1913, pp. 141-2.

32 Levy, pp. 263, 264.

33 *United Baptist Convention Year Book,* 1913, pp. 141-2.

34 *Year Book,* 1913, p. 141.

35 T.D. Denham, *History of the Germain Street Baptist Church, Saint John, N.B., One Hundred Years, 1810-1910* (Saint John, N.B., 1910), pp. 78-79.

36 *Year Book,* 1923 p. 150.

37 Levy, p. 225.

38 Denham, p. 70.

39 *Ibid.*, pp. 74-75.

APPENDICES

I

CONTRIBUTORS

ALLWOOD, Philip G. A., Minister, Seabright, Halifax Co., N.S. B0J 2Z0

DAVISON, James Doyle, Retired Minister and School Counsellor, Box 1092, Wolfville, N.S. B0P IX0

DEWEESE, Charles W., Director of Editorial Services, The Historical Commission of the Southern Baptist Convention, 127 Ninth Avenue, North, Nashville, Tennessee 37234

MOODY, Barry M., Assistant Professor, Department of History, Acadia University, Wolfville, N.S. B0P IX0

RAWYLK, George A., Professor, Department of History, Queen's University, Kingston, Ontario K7L 3N6

SINNOTT, Frank H., Minister, Box 86, Port Williams, N.S. B0P IT0

TRITES, Allison A., Associate Professor of Biblical Studies, Acadia Divinity College, Wolfville, N.S. B0P IX0

WILLIAMS, Savanah E., Lecturer, Department of Sociology and Anthropology, Dalhousie University, Halifax, N.S. (48 Cavendish Road, Halifax, N.S. B3P 2J7)

WRIGHT, Esther Clark, Historian, Wolfville, N.S. B0P IX0

BAPTISTS IN CANADA 1760-1980
International Symposium

Sponsored by
Acadia Divinity College

in co-operation with
The Baptist Federation of Canada and
Baptist Historical Committee of the United Baptist Convention
of the Atlantic Provinces

The Symposium includes the 1979 Hayward Lectures
presented as four public lectures in the evening sessions.

October 15-18, 1979
Wolfville, Nova Scotia

II

BAPTISTS IN CANADA

Other Published Essays

Other papers presented at the symposium "Baptists in Canada 1760-1980" at Acadia Divinity College, Wolfville, Nova Scotia, October 15-18, 1979, have appeared in the following publications and are available from the respective publishers, from the Baptist Resource Centre, 217 St. George Street, Toronto, Ontario, M5R 2M2, or from Baptist Bookroom, 101 Germain Street, Saint John, New Brunswick, E2L 2E9.

I BAPTISTS IN CANADA: Search for Identity amidst Diversity. Ed. Jarold K. Zeman. (G.R. Welch Co. Ltd., 960 Gateway, Burlington, Ontario L7L 5K7). 1980, $8.50.

Contents
PART ONE: INFLUENCES AND IDENTITY

W. Gordon Carder

PART THREE: THEOLOGICAL TRENDS AND
                       CONFLICTS

II **BAPTIST HISTORY AND HERITAGE,** Vol XV, No. 2 (April 1980). (127 Ninth Ave. N., Nashville, TN 37234). $1.50.

Contents

*Not presented at the Symposium.

III FOUNDATIONS, Vol 23, No. 1 (January-March 1980).
(18 Putnam Road, Arlington, MA 02174). $3.00.

Contents

IV. The paper on "Trends in Canadian Baptist Evangelism
Since World War II" by Thomas B. McDormand
appeared in *Expect a Difference: The Report Volume
of the Baptist Federation of Canada 1976-1979,* edited
by R.F. Bullen. It is available from Baptist Federation
of Canada, P.O. Box 1298, Brantford, Ontario, N3T
5T6.

V. The paper on "Thomas Todhunter Shields, Canadian
Fundamentalist" by C. Allyn Russell appeared in
Ontario History, Vol. 70 (1978): 263-280.